Note for Librarians: A cataloguing record for this book is available from Library and Archives Canada at www.collectionscanada.ca/amicus/index-e.html
ISBN 1-4251-0648-X

Offices in Canada, USA, Ireland and UK

Book sales for North America and international:
Trafford Publishing, 6E–2333 Government St.,
Victoria, BC V8T 4P4 CANADA
phone 250 383 6864 (toll-free 1 888 232 4444)
fax 250 383 6804; email to orders@trafford.com
Book sales in Europe:
Trafford Publishing (UK) Limited, 9 Park End Street, 2nd Floor
Oxford, UK OX1 1HH UNITED KINGDOM
phone +44 (0)1865 722 113 (local rate 0845 230 9601)
facsimile +44 (0)1865 722 868; info.uk@trafford.com
Order online at:
trafford.com/06-2406

10 9 8 7 6 5 4 3

"FOR THE WEAPONS OF OUR WARFARE"

UNDERSTANDING THE BASIC ATTACK TACTICS OF THE ADVERSARY AGAINST THE END-TIMES CHRISTIANS

"For this reason, I bow my knees before the Father, from whom every family in heaven and on earth takes its name. I pray that, according to the riches of his glory, he may grant that you may be strengthened in your inner being with power through his Spirit, and that Christ may dwell in your hearts through faith, as you are being rooted and grounded in love.

I pray that you may have the power to comprehend, with all the saints, what are the breadth and length and height and depth, and to know the love of Christ that surpasses knowledge, so that you may be filled with all the fullness of God.

Now to him who by the power at work within us is able to accomplish abundantly far more than all we can ask or imagine, to him be glory in the church and in Christ Jesus to all generations, forever and ever. Amen."

(Eph. 3:14-21)

"The Lord is my rock, my fortress and my deliverer; my God is my rock, in whom I take refuge. He is my shield and the horn of my salvation, my stronghold." (Psalm 18)

CONTENTS

CHAPTER 4

CHAPTER 5

CHAPTER 6

CHAPTER 7

CHAPTER 8

CHAPTER 9

AUTHOR'S ACKNOWLEDGEMENTS

FOR THE WEAPONS OF OUR WARFARE is not just the title of this book. It is a powerful caution by Apostle Paul on the aspects of spiritual warfare. It forms the bedrock of my survival in the harsh challenges of spiritual battlefield.

I wish to extend my deep and sincere gratitude to all my spiritual mentors who have assisted me in research, compilation and nailing together the pieces of this work.

The initial foundations to this work would have faltered without the hypercritical scrutiny by the Army Chaplains; Mr. Scott and Mr. John. Their profound knowledge and understanding of the scriptures remain a motivation to me in my quest for spiritual growth.

Special kisses of gratitude to my wife of eight years for the support and encouragement both during the writing as well as the editorial stages of this book. She is a true partner both in marriage and in Christ.

To my beloved daughters Alora, Alana, and Alexandra; thanks a million for exercising patience while your daddy spent times and moments away from you researching from the Bible and putting together the pieces of this book. You are my life impetus.

I also wish to acknowledge my mother for her steadfast and unwavering love and commitment to the Lord, which has guided me through my infancy stages in the Lord.

To my siblings and their families- Mr. Molefe, Mr. John-Gavin, and Mr. Campbell. Thank you for the moral and financial support you rendered me right from the conception stage until the full realization of this work.

The most creative and committed officer I have ever met has inspired my desire to study the military art of warfare. Mr. Eddie Molale remains my role model in commitment and knowledge of the profession of arms.

Special thanks to my beloved country Botswana, for developing me as an officer, a leader, and a responsible citizen.

Lastly, but certainly not least; my heartfelt gratitude to all the authors whose writings and in-depth coverage on the theory and conduct of warfare have inspired and assisted my work.

But to all the views, expressions, sentiments, assessments, over-tones and undertones; myself as the author of this book take the sole responsibility. God bless you al

PREFACE

"If you know the enemy and know yourself, you need not fear the result of a hundred battles. If you know yourself but not the enemy, for every victory gained you will also suffer a defeat. If you know neither the enemy nor yourself, you will succumb in every battle."

Sun Tzu-540 B.C

The spiritual warfare challenges are progressing at such a rapid and unprecedented magnitude, but the end-times church is seemingly oblivious of these last efforts of the adversary to conquer and defeat the potentially invincible children of the most High God.

The purpose of this book is therefore intended to simplify for easier comprehension the dynamics and complexities of spiritual warfare, and I have used as teaching aids the evolution of carnal warfare up to the contemporary era and its relationship with the spiritual warfare, and the fighting strategies and principles which I believe our adversary, the devil employs against God-fearing, born-again children of the Almighty God.

I have also utilized the military approaches to warfare as teaching aids for reference, relativity and easier comprehension of the spiritual fighting concepts and strategies that the devil uses against the church of Jesus Christ.

The object of this approach to spiritual warfare is for both the readers as well as practitioners of spiritual warfare to understand the thought process behind certain military tactics and/or strategies; the intended state of affairs that are desired as the end-state through the execution of such actions by the practitioners of carnal warfare, and how everything is all related and similar to the way our adversary skillfully fights us as Christians.

Once again, to answer the slowly-brewing question of why I have decided to utilize a militaristic approach?

Firstly, as a Christian military professional, it is the only approach that I know.

Secondly, you cannot divorce spiritual warfare from carnal warfare practices; the only and major difference between the two is the nature and means of conduct, but the application of the principles of warfare is similar and greatly intertwines.

Lastly, the scriptural imagery depiction of spiritual warfare by Saint Paul uses the military warfare language, and thus it is very appropriate to also discuss the theory and practicalities of warfare by using the commonly used terminologies and concepts that people can easily relate to in order to understand this very complex vocation.

Of greater interest for inclusion into this book is the advancement of the principles of spiritual attack strategies employed by our adversary the devil, which are aimed at defeating the church of Jesus Christ through the application of deceptive but very effective war-fighting strategies, rather than attempting to destroy us through incremental attrition.

From my personal spiritual standpoint and experience, I believe that the devil has co-opted and exploits what he knows man holds in high regard or is ignorant of, and uses that as a prodigious weapon to challenge and fight the church and the veracity of the Christian faith.

It is therefore necessary that every born-again Christian who is washed and redeemed by the blood, and is called into ministry, and seeks spiritual conquest, or even those other people who simply seek personal growth and subjugation in whatever facet of their lives should familiarize themselves with the basic fighting tactics and strategies of the devil, so that in our daily encounters with his scams we can use the authority we have in Jesus' name to completely bring his every effort under subjection.

I suppose that the inspiration to write this book is a long time challenge that I have for so long a time resisted. My approach to spiritual warfare is not intended to provide blanket solutions to the spiritual warfare challenges and encounters in our daily lives, because the focus of this book is on how I believe our adversary conducts his war-fighting business against the end-times Christians.

This book also does not claim to provide inestimable answers and solutions to our spiritual warfare problems, but is designed to serve as a spiritual caution, reference and awareness.

Lastly, this book does not claim any substitution to the Bible, and should only be used as a supplementary study aid. Because spiritual warfare is a very complex subject, it is only through the leading and revelation of the spirit of God that the subject of discussion of this book can be made intelligible to the readers who seek spiritual understanding, spiritual growth, spiritual maturity, and conquest.

Candidly speaking, I believe that the armies of God are potentially undefeatable and formidable; and I know for sure that the devil also is aware of this. How do I know that he knows? The Bible says that he was once a very resourceful and powerful archangel before his fall. He once had access to divine secrets.

"You were the anointed cherub who covers; I established you; you were on the holy mountain of God; you walked back and forth in the midst of fiery stones." (Ezekiel 28:14)

It therefore leaves us with no doubt that by having served God as the arch-angel at one time, Satan definitely knows our God's infinite supremacy. The devil is very much aware that he cannot resolutely attack and annihilate our spiritual lives; he simply attacks to destroy a Christian who is already spiritually vulnerable, defeated and weak.

As Christians, we should never regard Satan and his hosts as a bunch of clowns that can never provoke anything substantial in our spiritual lives. The devil is not as stupid as many Christians and non-Christians would like to think-or rather opt to deceive themselves; in fact the Bible in the book of Ezekiel 28:17 says that '*he was the seal of perfection, full of wisdom and perfect in beauty'*.

"Your heart was lifted up because of your beauty; thou hast corrupted thy wisdom by reason of thy brightness: I will cast thee to the ground, I will lay thee before kings, that they may behold thee."

He is therefore not this stupid, horned, fanged , ugly, hideous, and red-eyed humanoid creature as is usually sensationalized in church teachings. He carefully and meticulously plans his each and every effort, and chooses the right place and moment in our spiritual lives to attack. He knows that any direct and decisive confrontation with the children of God is suicidal and can only bring his scam to jeopardy. He attacks us at an opportune time, when our spiritual weaknesses are exposed.

The devil does not place much premium on any clean fight with the children of God. Since he knows that any protracted battles with the church would jeopardize chances of him achieving any spiritual gains, he therefore engages us in small, isolated but related spiritual skirmishes. He is a crafty tactician, and employs all his resources in the most economical way, ensuring that when he launches a limited-objective attack, he is assured and guaranteed localized victory.

CHAPTER 1

MY SPIRITUAL CONVICTIONS

"To win one hundred battles in one hundred wars is not the acme of skill, but to subdue your opponent without fighting is the supreme excellence"

-Sun Tzu (540 BC)

Spiritual warfare is a very old phenomenon, developed and fought very long time ago even before the times of creation. The spiritual being who opposes the church of God is Satan himself, and whose acts of rebellion and aggression date far back to the pre-creation period.

Satan in the Bible is likened to a thief who only comes to ***deceive***, to ***kill***, and to ***destroy*** (John 10:10).

The three definitive verbs should however be digested sparingly and with spiritual caution, because these are the creed upon which Satan's strategies are based. Deception is the tool or strategy- a mighty weapon that the devil uses with the over-all aim of misleading us so that we accept as true or valid what is false or invalid. This principal tool of deception shall form the backbone of our discussions later on in this book.

The Bible states that faith comes by hearing the word; and thus, the devil will do everything he can to deny us access to the word of God, he will oppose and nullify the integrity of the word of God, and in the process steals that which is rightfully ours.

Jesus says in John 17:17, ***"Thy Word is truth."***

Jesus goes on to say, ***"The world cannot accept Him*** (the Spirit of truth), ***because it neither sees Him nor knows Him ... But when He, the Spirit of truth, comes, He will guide you into all truth"*** (John 14:17; 16:13).

Therefore, it is the Spirit of Truth, whom the world <u>cannot</u> receive, that leads us into **ALL** truths. This is the underlying reason why the Spiritual element of the Triune God-Head is abominable in a lot of churches around the world, because Satan knows that it is only through the revelation character of the Spirit of God that the Bible ceases to exist as just a book of stories, and Christianity becomes a relationship with God and not just a religion or social past-time.

The Bible further gives us the assurance that it is through the knowledge of the Truth that we can be set free (John 8:32).

The big question is free from what? The Jews also asked Jesus similar question when he preached about the spiritual freedom in the book of John 8:33.

"We are Abraham's seed, and were never in bondage to any man: how then do you say, '***You shall be made free***?"

Jesus had answered them, '***Verily, verily, I say unto you, whosoever commits sin is the servant of sin.'*** (John 8:34)

The answer is very clear; if we arm our-selves with the knowledge of the truth in the word of God, we shall be set free from the bondage borne by ignorance of His Word; which can then easily be exploited by the adversary. This knowledge vacuum forms the core of the wiles and deceptive tactics of the devil.

Satan thus tries his level best to deny us knowledge of the truth about the word of God. In fact, some churches do not even encourage their followers to study the word of God outside the church environment, or even own the Bible for that matter. The followers only get to hear the word being preached at Church on Sundays.

How does one expect any growth in their spiritual lives when they only hear the word fifty-one days in a year, and expect spiritual conquest against spiritual attacks that average three-hundred and sixty-five days in a year? Don't we know that the Bible in its entirety as a package is designed to function in each single day of our lives until the day we die, whereupon we shall know the truth in full and would not need to read it anymore?

It was through the knowledge of the word of God that Jesus was able to resist and subsequently defeat the devil's temptations as well as his deceptive baits. In the book of Mathew 4:1-11, Jesus was led up by the Spirit into the wilderness to be tempted by the devil. He fasted for forty days and forty nights, and afterwards he was famished, experiencing a critical and vulnerable moment of his life.

In Mathew 4:3, the Bible says that the tempter approached and said to Jesus Christ; ***"If you are really the Son of God, command that these stones become loaves of bread."***

Jesus said this in reply, ***"It is written: 'One does not live by bread alone, but by every word that comes forth from the mouth of God."*** (Deuteronomy 8:1-6).

Then the devil took him to the holy city, and made him stand on the parapet of the temple, and said to him, "If you are the Son of God, throw yourself down. For it is written: ***'He will command his angels concerning you and 'with their hands they will support you, lest you dash your foot against a stone.'"*** (Psalms 91)

Jesus answered him, ***"Again it is written, 'Thou shall not put the Lord, your God, to the test."*** (Deuteronomy 12:4)

Then the devil took him up to a very high mountain, and showed him all the kingdoms of the world in their magnificence, and he said to him, "All these I shall give to you, if you will prostrate yourself and worship me."

At this point, Jesus said to him, ***"Get away, Satan! It is written: 'The Lord, your God, shall you worship and Him alone shall you serve."*** (Deuteronomy 5:7)

Then the devil left him and, behold, angels came and ministered unto him.

How many of us believers would have fallen for such a spiritual trap when Satan precisely quoted from the Bible? A lot of us would have taken it as the gospel truth! We probably would have been stupefied because we would be without any inherent knowledge of the most appropriate weapon to use against the appropriate target and at the appropriate range.

Can you imagine the situation of a soldier who is very much ill-informed about the enemy he is fighting, let alone the capabilities and limitations of his weapons against his adversary's capabilities? The poor soldier would open fire at an engagement range beyond the effective reach of his weapon, would engage a target that is not within the penetrating and destructive capability of his weapon. Do you know what would happen?

The enemy, being teased and angered by such an absurdity, would return fire and kill the poor soldier. This may seem trivial to some readers, but it constitutes the core in every country's basic military tactics.

I am always amazed and dismayed by those people who never read or study the scriptures, never attend worship, never hear the Word being preached, never fellowship with other Christians, and yet claim to have a close relationship with God.

How they can delude themselves, I often wonder. How can they be so misguided? How can they, how dare they claim a relationship with the Lord when there is no reading, studying, and preaching of the Word? How can they know Him that they do not know about?

They may be God's children, I do not refute that salvation fact, but they most certainly cannot have a growing and vibrant relationship with the Lord if they do not study and meditate in His Word. They also cannot know the appropriate weapon systems to employ or even defend effectively against the wide array of arsenals that the adversary employs against them.

Christianity is not a mechanized enterprise; God does not treat us like androids. In order to know the right weapon and response to our spiritual challenges, the word of God serves as the bricks and mortars, and the effective and efficient use of such assets is achieved through the relationship we have with Him. That is why Christianity is not a religion by definition; it is a relationship with God.

In the military profession, as a very basic soldiering skill; every soldier is required to know the nomenclature and technical data of the equipments and systems which he uses by heart. The poor soldier may have been a below-average student at school, but in the military he is sculptured to the required level of proficiency where he can recite with one hundred percent accuracy the capabilities and limitations of his weapons. He not only is required to know its capabilities and limitations, but also its correct tactical employment.

All of these he has to commit to heart, because he cannot keep on referring to the manufacture's manual during operation. This is the tactical formula for survival in the battlefield where time is of essence and targets are also equipped with equally capable weapons to engage you, and will definitely kill you if you do not kill them first.

Jesus did not keep on paging through the scrolls, looking for the appropriate scriptures that could neutralize Satan's efforts. He had donned on the word of God as sandals on his feet in preparation for the preaching of the gospel. We therefore, as his children and followers have to not only study the word of God, but should also meditate in it.

"I will meditate on all your works and consider all your mighty deeds. " (Psalms 77:12)

"I meditate on your precepts and consider your ways." (Psalms 119:15)

It therefore is also more than important for Christians to know the spiritual formula for survival against the fiery darts of the adversary. I often used to wonder why my church pastor made a big deal about a seemingly mundane thing such as not bringing a Bible to church, let alone a notebook and a pen to take notes during the preaching of the sermon. It has now become a standard procedure to the members of the Apostolic Faith Mission church to bring writing materials and Bibles to church.

This just goes to show how much importance is attached to the study of the word of God. Don't we bring or even provide such to our circular meetings? Or are we as Christians saying that the subject discussed in such meetings is of more importance to our lives than the truth shared during the preaching of the Word of God?

The Bible also tells us, ***"Resist the Devil and he shall flee from you"*** (James 4:7). To some Christians, this sounds very simplistic, unrealistic and perhaps very ambitious. The fact of the matter is, the verse is easier said than done.

How do you exactly resist an enemy when you are not even sure of his existence or aware of his operations? Some Christians do not even know who they are fighting! To them Satan and spiritual warfare are just the entertaining aspect of Christianity, or some form of scaremongering by preachers; they don't really relate the realities of spiritual warfare to the carnal warfare as we know or hear about it in day-to-day ***CNN*** or ***Fox News***' bulletins.

To some, the idea of resistance that the verse refers to is understood otherwise; they resist by calling Satan all sorts of names under the sun that describe every opposite and negative thing in life; they call him a liar, a thief, an adulterer, a fornicator, an instigator, a witch, a murder, etc.

I always wonder as to the effectiveness and impact on his operations by simply calling him all sorts of derogatory words when actually trying to bring down his strongholds!

Doesn't he know that he is a liar, a deceiver, or any of the evils schemes that truly describe his character? This is why a lot of our spiritual weaponry often mis-fires, it is because we are failing to comprehend even this minor spiritual craft. By simply calling out what best describes the devil does him absolutely no harm.

What do you think will happen to me if you were to start calling me a Christian, a soldier, an African, tall, etc? I would smile back and say, you bet I am exactly what you say I am!

The residual effect of this strategy, or should I say lack of strategy, is absolutely zero. The heart of covenantal prayer is the appeal to God's promises through prayer. In prayer, we ask God to do what He has promised He will do. We remind Him, so to speak, of His own words. The Lord's Prayer calls upon God to manifest the glory of His name, to bring in to this world His kingdom and to lead men to do His will on earth. This is the weapon that is very effective when dealing with Satan, it disrupts his efforts to deceive and mislead us of God's promises and will in our lives.

We should be spiritually conscious of what we say or do, and the spirit of God gives us such awareness and discernment. The devil disguises his activities; he diverts our attention on to his subterfuge, his evil surrogates, and his instruments of deception. He engages us in a spiritual wrestling duel, so that our efforts are directed only against the shadow and not the real object.

When talking about the aspect of spiritual warfare, some Christians justify their passiveness in the spiritual fight by saying that the Bible in the books of 1 Samuel 17:47 and 2 Chronicles 20:17 tells us that the ***battle is not ours to fight***, and that we should simply take our positions, stand still, and enjoy witnessing the victory of the Lord on our behalf. Lack of understanding of Gods grand strategy and plan makes us susceptible to attacks by the devil.

This in totality is exactly what he would like us to believe, so that in our passiveness and inactivity we oppose not his operations. We need to further establish and understand precisely what it is that God meant through the verse. We shall delve on this verse later in this book when we discuss God's design of battle.

I have often times inquired from a lot of my peer military professionals, and including Christian military officers as to what the actual purpose of warfare is. A lot would categorically answer that it is to kill the adversary and destroy his materials. The subject of the purpose of war is very confrontational, especially amongst aspiring strategists and military scholars. I have also had a discussion on the subject even with civilian Christians, and a lot have even accused me of heterodoxy.

This is where the misunderstanding of our core business and calling is, and unless we understand the object of spiritual warfare, we cannot effectively perform our specified duties as spiritual combatants. I don't however intend to delve much into this, or again start any confused and politicized discussions on the definition of war as may be defined by other professionals and critiques.

General War in the military dictionary is defined as an ***act of violence*** intended to ***compel*** our opponent to ***fulfill our will***. It is an act of ***forcing*** your opponent to ***yield to your will***, or to ***force him*** to ***agree on to your terms***.

This therefore, makes killing enemy soldiers and destroying his equipments simply the means to forcing him to agree to our terms.

The moment you give your life to Christ, you enter into a war with the world, which is more violent and bloodier than any of the carnal wars ever fought in world history. Satan and his hosts are at war with God and his children. Each opposing side strives to compel the other to yield to its will.

Apostle Paul says in the book of Ephesians 6:12 that ***"our struggle is not against enemies of flesh and blood, but against the rulers, against the authorities, against the cosmic powers of this present darkness, against the spiritual forces of evil in the heavenly places."***

This defines the threat against which Christians fight the spiritual wars. These in broad are our spiritual objectives.

I would like the term *objectives* as used throughout our discussions in this book to be understood as relating to the targets that need to be attacked and destroyed, rather than being the state of affairs that need to be achieved at the end of the war effort.

In order for the adversary to be reduced to a state of submission by an act of war, he must either be completely disarmed or placed in such a position that he is threatened with it. Many practitioners attack the acts of the devil and not the perpetrator of the acts himself.

In the book of Matthew 16:23, when Peter refused Jesus to return to Jerusalem because he knew that he would be crucified there; Jesus instead of rebuking Peter, rebuked Satan himself because he knew that it was not Peter but the devil who was behind that.

"But he turned, and said unto Peter, Get thee behind me, Satan: thou art an offence unto me: for thou savors not the things that be of God, but those that be of men."

In the book of Matthew 12:29, Jesus says that in order to destroy the works of the devil, he must be bound first.

"Or else how can one enter a strong man's house and plunder his goods, unless he first binds the strong man. That is when he can now plunder his house."

Can we take a one-second look at the following prayer of disarmament as an example, and perhaps we can understand exactly what I am talking about.

"Satan, it is written in the book of Psalms 91 ***that he who dwells in the shelter of the Most High, who abide in the shadow of the Almighty, will say to the Lord, 'my refuge and my fortress; my God in whom I trust.*** You and your hosts have no hold over my life, and you cannot reach out to me. I bind your every effort and with the authority of Jesus name, I bring your every act to subjection and to the obedience of God. I bring into disarray your cohesion, and confuse your every action with the power in Jesus name. The spirit of sexual immorality, promiscuity, adultery, fornication, idolatry, witchcraft, racism, corruption, sickness; I destroy your holds in the name of Jesus. I take authority against the spirit of pride, and command it to the obedience of

God...."

It therefore follows that the disarming of the adversary that will in turn lead to his submission must always be the aim of our warfare. Paul thus defines the object or purpose of our warfare very succinctly in 2 Corinthians 10:5.

"......to destroy arguments and every proud obstacle that exalts itself against the knowledge of God, and to take into captivity every thought to the obedience of Christ."

Lastly, in order to defeat the adversary, we must proportion our efforts to his powers of resistance. Apostle Paul has defined explicitly what we fight against, and approximated the strength of the powers and forces we have to contend with. He reviews our only spiritual means of waging war in the book of Ephesians 6:10-18.

"Finally, be strong in the Lord and in his mighty power. Put on the full armor of God so that you can take your stand against the devil's schemes."

If the carnal enemy is armored, battle-filed commonsense would tell us that we should employ our amour or tanks, as well as anti-armor weapons systems to destroy him. Likewise, with our spiritual enemy, the Holy Spirit of God gives us the discernment and utterance of the appropriate spiritual weapons in the Word of God to destroy the acts of the devil.

In order to live a life of victory in the Lord, we need to also fully understand the meaning and implications of the word of God in Ephesians 6:11-18 11 when it says through Paul.

"Finally, be strong in the Lord and in the power of His might. Put on the whole armor of God, so that you may be able to stand against the wiles of the devil.".......... "Therefore take up the whole armor of God, so that you may be able to withstand in the evil day, and having done all, to stand. Stand therefore, <u>having girded your waist with truth</u>, <u>having put on the breastplate of righteousness</u>, and having <u>shod your feet with the preparation</u> of the gospel of peace; above all, <u>taking the shield of faith</u> with which you will be able to quench all the <u>fiery darts of the wicked one</u>."

Before we can even start discussing the basic strategies and tactics of our adversary, it needs to be absolutely clear in our minds what Apostle Paul meant by the scriptures, because some Christians would literally wear church attires and carry some forms of weaponry in utter believe that they are satisfying exactly what Paul prescribed as the spiritual protection against the acts of aggression of the adversary.

Let us take the underlined statements one-by-one for easier comprehension. If we can understand these, as I know God will help us to understand, then we should not have problems understanding the strategies of our adversary later on in our discussions.

In Ephesians 6:14 Christians are exhorted to put on **"the breastplate of righteousness**," as protection against Satanic attacks. At the time that Apostle Paul wrote the scriptures, the breastplate was the most important piece of protection for a Roman soldier to wear in order to survive in the battlefield of those times. It protected his heart area, and other vital organs from the darts or spears thrown by the adversary. We still use the breast plate even in modernized armies of the contemporary era, except that it is now much lighter and is called body amour or bullet-proof jacket or vest!

But what significance does the "breastplate of righteousness" have for believers *now?* Without God on our side, we are without any form of protection against attacks from the devil. Attacks should be understood in the broader sense, because the word of God (I believe) refers to spiritual attacks and not physical attacks, and I will advance reasons later on in our discussions on the topic.

The carnal battlefield is not orchestrated to be geographically even like a play ground; it is full of all types of obstacles which are in turn exploited by the adversary; there are those that are man-made and those that are cultural. Regardless of the type of obstacles, the bottom line is that they impede our activities and interfere with our freedom of action.

Likewise, even in our spiritual walks we also have a spiritual enemy, and our lives are not about level ground, but about keeping our faith in the midst of adversity, regardless of the spiritual terrain we operate in. God has deliberately allowed us to function in such an environment in order to bring about spiritual discipline and growth. Anyone in a battle situation must have surefootedness or stability to avoid falling and becoming defenseless. Anyone can walk on level ground, but our enduring spirit is really tested in the mountains, water, fire, sharp rocks, ice, fatigue, scorching heat, wind, etc.

Paul continues his comparison of the amour of God and the Roman amour with the shield. For the Roman soldier of those times, his amour protection was a very large, oblong, four-cornered shield that could easily block any arrow, spear, or javelin aimed at the soldier. It was as large as a door. It was made of wood the surface of which was hardened and then covered with leather.

A soldier could hide his whole body behind this shield and be absolutely safe. Without the shield, he was vulnerable to any and all sorts of missiles aimed and hurled at him. A Christian also has a shield; and that shield is faith, which stands between us and the many attacks and temptations that we face every day.

When Satan throws a situation, let us say a medical condition as an example, we parry it off with the scriptures;

".....Satan, it is written that he bore our infirmities and healed our diseases." (1 Peter 2:24-25)

All the activities that the Bible through Paul says we should perform are all oriented at defeating only one thing, and that is <u>the fiery darts of the wicked one</u>- and this wicked one is Satan himself and his hosts. Without such a spiritual condition, there would be no requirement of a combat posture, because there would be absolute peace.

If you watch old war movies, especially the Roman wars, you would appreciate the type of arrows the soldiers used at the times Apostle Paul wrote his books. The Roman forces used flaming missiles to destroy their enemies. The "fiery darts" which the Bible through Paul refers to in this passage were made from a hollow reed, and its end was blocked and the reed filled with a flammable liquid. A loosely fitting stopper holding a wick was slipped into the other end of the tube and lit. It was then shot like an arrow at the enemy soldier. When it hit a soldier, the wick popped out, the flammable liquid spilled over the soldier's armor and ignited, literally roasting him in his own amour. Just like any missile used even by contemporary forces, you cannot see it coming towards you, but the results are very devastating.

This is a true depiction of Satan's tactics. He sends something our way - a thought, a doubt, and an unholy idea, which may seem very innocent at first, but when it strikes it spreads its destruction throughout our spiritual lives engulfing us in his satanic flames. It attracts other spiritual problems, which we are inevitably forced to contend with.

In as much as we know or are aware of the activities of the adversary, a lot about his operations or his schemes and tactics is however unknown to us and falls within the domain of the spiritual abstract. Without the discernment character of the Spirit of God, our war efforts would not bear fruit because what cannot be seen cannot be attacked, and what cannot be attacked cannot be destroyed; what cannot be destroyed cannot be drawn to submission. We therefore require the divine intelligence so that our efforts are rendered relevant and effective in the spiritual fight.

In carnal structures, war is inarguably an extension of the national Political will. It is however not just merely a political act, but also a real political instrument, a continuation of political commerce, a carrying out of the same through military means. It must be noted that the Grand or Political strategy defines how the nation intends to employ all its resources (not only the military forces) in pursuance of national goals.

In the book of Mathew 11:12, the Bible says;

"From the days of John the Baptist until now the kingdom of heaven suffers violence, and violent men take it by force."

From John's initial announcement of the coming of the Kingdom of God, the response had been a violent one by those who were opposed to the preaching of the coming Kingdom of God. There are so many people today who are working day in and day out to try to vilify the core integrity and truth about God, and so many nations are fighting against Christianity. These are the 'last kicks of a dying horse', the devil knows very well that his time is finally closing to a dead end, and he is desperately trying to subvert our loyalty to the cause.

In the context of our warfare, beyond these carnal structures which Apostle Paul refers to which pertains to us spiritual combatants, is related strictly to the peculiar nature of the divine means of achieving God's will through the involvement and employment of Christians in spiritual warfare.

Since the political view or goal is the object, then war is the means of achieving it, and the means (war) must always include the object (Political view) in its concept and conduct. If this is ignored, then the army fights in complete isolation and will not achieve its national goals.

The will of God therefore forms the core object of our faith and salvation, and spiritual warfare is simply the means of attaining it.

"Therefore do not be foolish, but understand what the Lord's will is." (Ephesians 5:17)

Without understanding the will of God it is impossible to fulfill the mission of our calling. We simply act on impulses, and fight uncoordinated, leaderless, as well as un-resourced battles. Jesus Christ in the book of Mark 14:32 (also Matthews 26:36 and Luke 22:39) when he was with the disciples at the garden of Gethsemane prayed that God's will be done, and not his. He said this in Verse 36;

"Father, for you all things are possible; remove this cup from me; yet not my will but your will be done."

This is why the spirit of God informed Jahaziel of Judah that the battle was not Judah's but the Lord's, and told the army of Judah about God's plan for their participation and their deployment positions and role in the overall posture of the war plan.

The book of 1 Samuel 17:46 says;

"This day will the LORD deliver thee into mine hand; and I will smite thee, and take thine head from thee; and I will give the carcasses of the host of the Philistines this day unto the fowls of the air, and to the wild beasts of the earth; that all the earth may know that there is a God in Israel."

In the book of 1 Samuel 17:47, David explains the purpose of the fight;

"And all this assembly shall know that the LORD saves not with the sword and spear: for the battle is the Lord's, and he will give you into our hands."

In this scripture, David was about to engage his opponent in physical duel. He appreciated the fact that through all the challenges that lied ahead of him, God was going to lead him through the situation. He also appreciated the fact that he was not fighting the battle for his own gains, and that he was simply being utilized as the means to achieving God's will. The purpose of his fight against the armies of Philistia was to fulfill the scriptures that there is no other god but Jehovah God.

Don't we think that God could have just killed Goliath without David having to do it? Just a heart attack would have done the job without any spillage of blood. Once again, if it was the will of God, then salvation could still have been fulfilled even without Jesus Christ having had to go through the crucifixion.

My argument on this issue of passivity therefore is, if as Christians we have no role to play at all in the spiritual battles, why would God again through Paul tell us to put on the amour in preparation for war? Why would the president tell non-combatants to put on their combat gear and ready themselves for war? It just would not make any sense at all. Only soldiers fight.

We often sing the song 'I am a soldier in the Army of the Lord!' I guess according to some of us, we see ourselves as civilians wearing and putting on our combat gears and being launched into battle without a role to play! We look at ourselves simply as a bunch of Christian performers and bystanders; we sing for the sake of it. This is utterly absurd, I am sorry to say this.

Even in carnal perspective, any military force engaged in war would not claim to be fighting its own war, but the nations! When the army fights, it fights the national war, and not its own. Likewise, when there is war, the nation is said to be at war! In military operations, the political and military strategic level commander's *intent* and *will* are always repeated to assist subordinate leaders to function within the confines that such may impose on mission execution.

The United States Department of Defense defines the Commander's Intent as 'a concise expression of the <u>purpose of the operation</u> and the <u>desired end state</u> that serves as the initial impetus for the planning process.

Jahaziel therefore also needed a reminder from God that even though he had chosen the forces of Judah to fight the battle, it was however not theirs but the Lord's to fight. God could have destroyed the enemies of Judah without their involvement. God can also heal us, protect us, and bless us. There is however one condition, we have to claim all these through prayer and supplication.

God wants us as his children to claim the victory by invoking the name of Jesus and watch him win it for us, as simple as that. We need to claim all His promises according to His Word.

Jehovah as the omniscient God does not assess a situation on a narrow and tunnel vision scope. He provides us with very succinct guidance as to our roles and functions in the fight. This is why it is absolutely imperative that we hear from him before we embark in any combat undertakings. What do you think would have happened if the army of Judea had not sought God's guidance, and instead attacked using their human intellect? The results would have been very disastrous in terms of human losses.

Think about this; just as in carnal campaign design, God as the Commander-in-Chief as well as our military commander sets the conditions under which we are to wage war as his spiritual soldiers; he directs our every move in order to ensure that every spiritual situation is dealt with effectively and accordingly in a synchronized and coordinated manner. He provides the required spiritual support so that we can defeat every opposition through the authority of his name.

Through His discerning Spirit He provides us with insights to the spiritual objectives (prayer items) to be attacked so that we are not barking at the wrong tree. He sustains us (so that we stay motivated to serve Him) when we are tired, weary, wounded, and famished. He restores our hope when the situation seems hopeless (so that we don't shirk our duties).

He guides our every move so that we can tread on serpents without being bit. We are combatants for heaven's sake, and it is high time Christians wake up and assume their rightful positions in the broad spectra of the disposition of heavenly forces.

CHAPTER 2

THE EVOLUTION OF CARNAL WARFARE

"For though we live in the world, we do not wage war as the world does. The weapons we fight with are not the weapons of the world. On the contrary, they have divine power to demolish strongholds. We demolish arguments and every pretension that sets itself up against the knowledge of God, and we take captive every thought to make it obedient to Christ."

-2 Corinthians 10:3-5

Primitive clashes of force occurred very long time ago, when groups of Pre-Historic combatant men, armed with crude stone implements, fought with other groups for food, women, or land. Somewhere again along the pre-historic road, other drives- such as sport, the urge for dominance, or the desire for independence-became further causes for armed conflicts.

The dawn of history and the beginning of organized warfare went hand-in-glove. Most primitive societies learned the use of metals at the same time that they developed a system of writing. This phenomenon appeared almost simultaneously and apparently quite independently; in Mesopotamia and Egypt sometime between 3500 and 3000 B.C, when the use of copper for weapons, household implements, and decorations began.

Several hundred more years elapsed before men mastered the secret of hardening copper into bronze by mixing tin with it. Comparable developments of Bronze Age culture occurred in the Indus Valley sometimes before 2500 B.C and in the Yellow River Valley of China presumably several centuries later. Iron metallurgy began to replace bronze in the Middle East shortly before 1000B.C and in Europe soon thereafter. It was a few centuries later when the Iron Age appeared in India and China.

The ancient history which began with Bronze Age cultures is known to us largely in terms of military history, when accounts of who conquered who were narrated. The record is almost entirely devoted to migrations, wars, and conquests. Not until about 1500

B.C, however, are we able to visualize the actual course of any of the constant wars in the Middle East Asia, or dimly to perceive primitive military organizations and methods of combat. By the 6th Century B.C, relatively comprehensive and more or less continuous records of wars became available.

WEAPONS

"For the weapons of our warfare are not carnal, but mighty through God to the pulling down of strongholds. We destroy argument, and every obstacle that raises itself against the knowledge of God, and we take every thought captive to obey Christ" (2 Corinthians 10:4)

PRIMITIVE WEAPONS

Primitive weapons fell into two major categories; shock and missile. The two categories are now broadly classified into Kinetic Energy and Chemical Energy ammunitions. Kinetic Energy ammunitions generally depend on their built-in mass and speed to effect target destruction. The Chemical Energy ammunition, on the other hand depend on their built-in chemical compound and not speed and mass, to destroy a target.

The original shock weapon was the prehistoric man's club; the first missile weapon was the rock that man hurled at hunted prey or human enemy. The next important development was the leather sling or catapult for hurling small, smooth rocks with greater force for larger distances than was possible by arm power alone. In some regions the rock gradually was displaced by a light club, or throwing stick, which in turn evolved into darts, javelins, and the boomerang.

The club was later modified in a number of other ways, including the spiky head for greater lethality. The shock-action counterpart of the javelin was the heavy pike, or thrusting spear. The basic club itself took on a variety of forms, of which the Native American tomahawk is an example, while clubs with sharpened edges became Stone Age prototypes of the sword. The bow, developed late in the Stone Age, was also invaluable to early fighting man and to his successors over many centuries.

The most important form of protective amour devised by primitive man was the shield, which was designed to be held almost in many cases in the left hand, or on the left arm, leaving the right arm free to wield a weapon. Shields most often were simple wooden frameworks, covered with leather hides, though some were made entirely of hide as was the case in African Regiments.

HISTORIC WEAPONS

The most important weapons improvement during the early Historic period was the adoption of metal for the points, edges, or smashing surfaces in the Bronze and Iron Ages.

The first new weapons of the metallic era were the dagger, then the sword. The long thin blade which characterizes the sword could not have been created until metallurgy had sufficiently been developed to permit the working of hard malleable metal. This occurred in the Bronze Age sometimes before 2000 B.C, and the sword was reportedly introduced into the warfare by the Assyrians.

Protective body amour was also greatly improved during the Bronze Age. Although leather remained the basic and most common material, this was often reinforced with metals; some helmets, breastplates, and greaves were entirely in metal-at first bronze, later iron.

MODERN WEAPONS

Modern warfare is a formidable display of technological expertise and innovation in weapons development. There has been a great advent in technology as regards weapons of the contemporary era. The force modernization program administrators are working around the clock to develop very sophisticated weapons with smart munitions capable of engaging targets beyond visual ranges.

Mankind possesses the technology and profound ingenuity to develop any formidable weapon system unimaginable; in fact mankind has developed Nuclear, Biological, and Chemical energy weapons that have the capability to obliterate the entire globe in a fraction of a second. The desire to dominate and conquer has been the driving force to weapon system development by the great nations of the world today.

The improvements in weapon systems and the developments of smart munitions have however not changed the biological make-up of the soldier who fights the war. Even though the modern day soldier is more educated, highly trained, and well equipped; his reaction to the element of fear and killing however remains almost invariably the same as the olden times soldier. A Stone-Age soldier experienced fear just like the modern soldier, he equally gets fatigued and shirks duty just the same.

This therefore makes it an aspect of interest in evaluating our design of battle as the children of God and the devil's scheme of operation as the opposing force to the church of Jesus Christ. A spiritual warfare practitioner during the times of the Bible experienced similar challenges as the spiritual warfare practitioners of the contemporary age.

Some Christians often claim that the kind of spiritual warfare that Christians fought during the times of the Bible is outdated, as the world has presumably changed. This is a wrong assessment and conclusion, because the world has not changed at all; it is only the situations and conditions that have changed. Some would even claim that the civilization of mankind has created an utopist environment, and that mankind is at absolute peace with the environment.

Let us wake up and smell the coffee, because the constant progress of improvements in the design of carnal weapons as I have already elucidated, are sufficient proofs that the tendency to destroy the adversary which lies at the bottom of the conception of war has in no way changed or modified our perception of the state of peace through the progress of civilization.

How come then, when we now think about spiritual warfare we tend to deceive ourselves into believing that civilization has brought about a reduction in the resistance and rivalry efforts of the adversary? We are now wiser than our forefathers, and by professing to be wise, we have literally become as fools. Do we really believe that military technology makes a contemporary soldier any better that olden times soldier? Read a lot on military losses of even the most technologically advanced armies of the world. Spiritual warfare is not of any less significance or complexity than carnal warfare; it is a serious and more complex call than the military's. To understand it, we need the Spirit of God, because He is the only means of unlocking the mysteries of the Bible and making it intelligible to us.

CHAPTER 3

UNDERSTANDING OUR SPIRITUAL ADVERSARY

"Before I took a decision or adopted an alternative, it was after studying every relevant- and many an irrelevant factor. Geography, tribal structure, religion, social customs, language, appetites, and standards-all were at my fingertips. The enemy I knew almost like my own side."

T.E Lawrence (Arabia), 1933

A person who claims to be a combatant soldier but is ignorant of the enemy he is fighting ought to call himself a civilian dressed up in military uniform. He does not understand his calling. The same applies to a Christian who focuses only on the ultimate Glory, and is ignorant of all the obstacles that lie on his way that may impede his advance and growth. The works of the devil are nothing but spiritual obstacles that try to deny us spiritual growth. They distract us from focusing on God, and in many cases will try to divert our attention so that by doing so he trades growth for time.

If such an entity as Satan really exists, it really doesn't matter much whether we think that it is harmful to conceive of Satan the way we do without risking provoking a hostile response by him; or if we think we would be more at peace with ourselves and the devil if we ditch the idea of an entity behind the malevolence against the children and the Church of God; or worse still if we think the human race should learn to adapt to such challenges and accept them as merely simple co-existing natural phenomenon.

What matters most is not what you and I think, but what the Bible says. The Bible categorically and without compromise, warns us that this entity actually exists. And since it does exist, then all those intelligent, rational thoughts take us away from really focusing on the object but instead its shadow. The wisdom of man is just so much stupidity with God, and the Bible says in the book of Romans 1:22 that ***'even though we profess to be wise, we have become as fools.'***

As a combatant, before you can put on your combat gear, equip yourself with all the mission-essential items and equipments, and ready yourself to execute your attack plan; you need to understand the sphere within which your adversary operates, and his geographic dispositions and dispensations.

You should know Satan's tactics, techniques, strong points and strongholds, activities of his hosts and the physical or spiritual realms where they exist and function. Even in carnal warfare, intelligence which is simply an understanding about your enemy, the battlefield terrain as well as the environment you shall be fighting in is very critical and crucial to mission success.

Likewise, God has given the spiritual combatants a character that is more efficient than any of the intelligence collection and processing systems of the world; we have the Spirit of God Who guides our every effort in battle!

"But when He, the Spirit of truth comes, he shall teach you all truths. For he shall not speak of himself, but what things He so ever He shall hear, He shall speak; and the things that shall come, He shall show you." (John 16:13)

The devil's sphere of operation is not unlimited, and God has purposely designed it so that from our positions and dispositions, we can bring down all our spiritual authority and might to bear against all his efforts whilst at the same time staying away from the radius of reach of his weapons. God has designed parameters within which the devil can wage his war, and proportioned his resistance according to our spiritual maturity and capabilities.

"There is no temptation taken you but such as is common to man: but God is faithful, who will not suffer you to be tempted above that you are able; but will with the temptation also make a way to escape, that you may be able to bear it." (1 Corinthians. 10:13)

A trial could come upon us not necessarily because of anything that we did or because something is wrong with us, but one could come upon us from this world or from Satan. As human beings living in this world, the trials that come upon us Christians are the same as occur to all men. As we live life, we find that in most cases these trials are unavoidable. They just happen. If it happens to the world, we are part of what is going on in the world, and these things affect us unavoidably.

The only difference that we have with the world is through the assurance God gives us that He will provide "*the* way of escape," implying that there is one right way out of each trial. There may be other optional ways, but Paul is stressing that there is "a way" and "the way." We want "the way," the one that God provides for us.

God promises flat out that He will never allow us to be tempted above what we are able to handle, and that He will always provide a way of escape. In God, we are not without resources to overcome whatever challenges we may be faced with in life.

A fighter who does not understand the effectiveness of his adversary's weapons cannot effectively appreciate their capabilities, and therefore cannot effectively plan to defeat such weapons. A spiritual fighter needs to understand that the devil and his devilish hosts have limited capability to affect us in any number of ways. The good thing to note, again, is that when they attack, it is because our sovereign Commander Jesus Christ has permitted them to test us or to chastise us within the established confines.

THE FUNCTIONS OF SATAN'S HOSTS

Satan is a skilled commander, who once commanded the angelic armies of the sovereign God. His understanding of tactics and war-fighting strategies is impressively impeccable. He as the commander does not do the dirty job all alone and by himself; he has his devilish hosts that execute the plan for him. The hosts perform the following tasks;

They can influence our thoughts with temptations. In Acts 5:3, a certain man named Ananias, with Sapphira his wife sold their possession, and kept back part of the price. But Peter said, "Ananias, why has Satan filled your heart to lie to the Holy Ghost, and to keep back part of the price of the land?"

The fact is, the initial battle is that of the mind. As a tactician, you will, in many cases think, plan, and function according to your perception of the situation. The same applies with our spiritual encounters, if we function by the flesh.

They can influence and control our dream state - nightmares. (Job 4:12-16).

"Now a thing was secretly brought to me, and mine ear received a little thereof. In thoughts from the visions of the night, when deep sleep falls on men, fear came upon me, and trembling, which made all my bones to shake."

How many people have fallen into traps and snares laid by the devil through dreams? This is the reason why so many people even maintain ties with ancestral spirits.

They are able to cause emotional, mental or physical trauma (fear, confusion & pain).

They erect spiritual barriers or walls in our lives and relationships. This is known as spiritually isolating the target. It is easier to successfully attack and destroy an isolated Christian than the one who is mutually supportive with others in terms of prayer or one that is spiritually self-supportive. Thus, the object of Satan creating barriers in our lives is to cut off any relationship and communication we have with God, and subsequently attack and destroy us peace meal.

They sometimes affect our health. (Job 2:7)

"So Satan went forth from the presence of Yahweh, and struck Job with painful sores from the sole of his foot to his head."

The fact is, as humans our threshold for pain and suffering differs, and Satan believes that people will instantly give away all that they have in order to save their lives from momentary suffering or pain (Job 2:4)

Their greatest effectiveness is when they stay veiled and people start to think that their problems are natural ones. I wish to hasten to disclaim any suggestion that people, and Christians for that matter, should treat each and every incident that happens in their lives as being the work of the devil.

On the contrary, I am not encouraging any battlefield common sense, as is the case in many carnal military teachings. The discerning character of the Spirit of God provides the spiritual situation awareness that we require as a pre-requisite for survival in the spiritual battlefield.

A spiritual warrior has spiritual alertness to the activities of the enemy. This alertness is by no means borne of fear or paranoia. He does not go around crediting Satan and his hosts for everything wrong under the sun.

The Apostle Paul was a good example of a spiritual warrior. He didn't go out of his way to look for demonic activities, but when he encountered any, he quickly recognized it and then confronted it with the spiritual authority he had in Jesus, and victoriously bringing it under subjection.

As a warrior, you should also have a sense of situational awareness; you should understand where you are and where you are going, and all the factors that can either affect or influence your success in battle.

WHO REALLY IS SATAN?

Satan is a frustrated being, whose primary aim is to assert his influence and turn everybody against God and His divine promises, because he knows beyond a shadow of doubt that he is destined for doom. Thus says the Lord GOD in the book of Isaiah 14:12-14:

"You were the seal of perfection, full of wisdom and perfect in beauty. You were in Eden, the garden of God; every precious stone was your covering: the sardius, topaz, and diamond, beryl, onyx, and jasper, sapphire, turquoise, and emerald with gold. The workmanship of your timbres and pipes was prepared for you on the day you were created."

So, what kind of a character do the scriptures tell us about this evil being who commands opposing forces to God and Christians? The devil is portrayed as having the will, the ability, and much supernatural powers, even if the powers come mostly from his skill at lies and deceit. Satan has an identity and a purpose (or anti-purpose). Satan is an instigator, an insurrectionist, and a reactionary, he is the one who starts fights and the one whose reason for warfare is to frustrate and obstruct God's Kingdom in every way.

The Devil is more than a match for any person standing on his or her own, or for that matter any group of human beings who rely on their strengths and not the Lord's. We are no match for Satan on our own because we are out of defensive reach from the only One (God) who has the power to defeat Satan. Christ, by coming into the created world, has blatantly declared Satan's acts as bluffs and flushes him out from everywhere he lurks in our lives.

"Blessed is the Nation Whose God is the Lord" (Psalm 33:12).

The Devil is not an anti-god. The Devil is more like a god with a small 'g'; a face without a person behind it, all apparitions and no substance. He does not deny God's existence as God or his omni-presence, omni-potency, and his omniscience characteristics. He however wants people to look at God and himself as two co-existing godheads.

"How you are fallen from heaven, O Lucifer, son of the morning! How you are cut down to the ground, you who weakened the nations! For you have said in your heart: 'I will ascend into heaven, I will exalt my throne above the stars of God; I will also sit on the mount of the congregation on the farthest sides of the north; I will ascend above the heights of the clouds, I will be like the Most High.' (Isaiah 14.12-14)

His ultimate end-state is to see many people joining his corrupt little empire and perishing with him in hell. Why do you think that even though many people and religions believe and know that there is

God, many still refuse to honor Him as God and serve only Him; but they have instead become futile in their thinking, and their senseless minds are darkened by their acts (Romans 1:21-23).

The Hindu teachings claim that Jesus was taught by Buddhist monks for the 18 years of his life in India before he started his ministry in the Middle-East. They claim that he performed miracles because of the supposedly skills he acquired through yoga. They also acknowledge the fact that Jesus was crucified, but they refute the truth about his resurrection, claiming that he was rescued by some traders who took him to Kashmir where he later died at a ripe age. This is Satan's attempt to create confusion in order to mislead the masses.

Islam in its teachings does not refute the fact that Jesus could heal the sick and the suffering, but it teaches that he was just a 'mere' prophet.

Satan can tempt and lie to us, but can never fully do so. He requires God's permission first in order to tempt us! Satan, like the archangel he once was, can't make us do anything really without God's permission.

Martin Luther in his writings likened Satan to a snarling dog that is chained in place to a pole for restraint, and who can only do you real harm if you're foolish enough to come too close within his radius of effectiveness.

All Satan can do is use cunning tricks to play off our weaknesses and circumstances, to lead us to choose to do things, which suck the life, hope, and dignity out of ourselves. And each time we do that, we lose the image and character of God and reflect only his character and image.

Unfortunately, some Christians would rather not talk about the effect of Satan in their spiritual walks. The Satan talk turns them off, or they just think that Satan is just a construct or a symbol that churches or even pastors created to show just how humans tend toward evil, and is used as some form of scare-mongering to make us live responsibly.

Some would even suggest that only those people who are academically bankrupt would believe that Satan really exists. Some would even claim that Satan is only operational in Africa and Asia!

This is the stupidest of the stupidest thinking; Satan's targets are not races and continents, but human beings across the globe regardless of gender, ethnicity, social status or education.

The devil is very much aware of this, and so he controls a good chunk of the academic arena. It is only the educated masses who would believe the devil's lies that man evolved from apes, and that everything came into being through the Big-Bang process.

Ask any illiterate in the streets, they will unanimously proclaim that God created man and everything on earth without necessarily going through the hermeneutics of theology.

The evolution misinformation is meant to create an equalizer to Gods process of creation by the devil and his academic hosts.

The Big Bang Theory is the dominant scientific theory which is intended to corrupt and challenge the gospel of Jehovah God's creation of the universe. According to the Big Bang, the universe was created sometime between 10 billion and 20 billion years ago from a cosmic explosion that hurled matter in all directions. What absurdity!

In 1927, the Belgian priest named Georges Lemaître was the first to propose that the universe began with the explosion of a primeval atom. The fact is that there are billions out there who actually believe in this spiritually bankrupt sorry excuse of scientific explanation.

Satan is a defeated foe, and all he is doing at the moment is to employ propaganda in order to subvert our loyalty to God so that we can defect to his faction. He has schemes that he employs to lure, and subsequently destroy us. Any dealings or contracts with him are costly, and the covenant is suicidal.

CHAPTER 4

THE PSYCHOLOGY OF WARFARE

"But they that wait upon the LORD shall renew their strength; they shall mount up with wings as EAGLES. They shall run, and not be weary; and they shall walk, and not faint."

(Isaiah 40:31)

Of greater interests and fascination in my studies throughout my noble military career are the military fighting concepts and strategies of General Sun Tzu. Sun Tzu was a Chinese General who was born and raised in the state of Chi at around 540 B.C, and eventually lived in the kingdom of Wu, where he gained the favor of the King. For nearly twenty years, Sun Tzu led the armies of the King in a series of successful wars through the employment of war-fighting strategies, which still inspire many military scholars of the contemporary age.

He wrote many books during the fifth century B.C, and his writings have influenced the development of Eastern and Asian military thought throughout history.

Proponents of both conventional and unconventional tactics have pointed to the basic wisdom and principles developed by Sun Tzu. His military and political thought has influenced many great nations (including the Soviet Union and Peoples Republic of China) of the contemporary era. The royal United Kingdom and the great United States of America have also of recent embraced his teachings in their new war fighting strategies in order to be effective in the contemporary operational environment.

One of the greatest emphases in General Sun Tzu's book titled '**The Art of War**' is upon the human psychology in war. He believed that the human mind and soul play a critical role in the conduct of warfare. All wars, spiritual or canal are won and lost in the minds of man. Although he was not learned in any of the highly recognized institutions of the modern age, and did not possess the fully developed science and knowledge of the human soul and mind as we have today; his approach to the science and art of warfare was impeccable. Sun Tzu delved a lot on the aspects of deception, the morale, and the expectations of the adversary.

Furthermore, he made it clear to students of warfare that defeat is essentially a psychological phenomenon, rather than quantifiable 'body counts'. The loss of a battle is not necessarily the loss of a war. Thus Sun Tzu captures this in his famous quote.

"An army is defeated not through incremental attrition of its physical components, but only when its will to continue the struggle is lost."

The will power or enduring spirit, which is essentially a psychological state of mind, is the driving force to perseverance and victory in battle. The primary target of the devil is also not on the physical aspect of the human being, but rather on the mind-or the spirit.

The devil is a great fabricator of lies, and he changes the truth of the Almighty God into his lies (Roman 1:25). His aim is to make us serve him. This explains why there are many cults and occults that have subjected their followers to so much spiritual bondage, and the oppressed do not even realize it as oppression. Why do you think countries that serve and worship idols have got a lot of bad stuff in the bag to contend with?

In some Asian countries people would rather die of poverty; they can neither sell nor eat beef simply because a cow or another animal is worshiped as god.

Surprisingly though, they can beat it, harness it, make it work, and do all sorts of things but to eat it is considered unholy.

In many households or street corner in Asia for example, people have designed images of persons, cows, and elephants that that they worship as god. The devil has invariably made such countries his stronghold, his operating base. The poor are getting poorer by the day, and those who design and manufacture these idols get richer by the day.

Demetrius the silversmith, in the book of Acts 19:26-27 solicited support from fellow silversmiths and citizens against Apostle Paul's efforts when he vehemently preached against such idol worship.

In the book of Acts 19 verse 26 he says.

"Moreover you see and hear, that not only alone in Ephesus, but almost throughout all Asia, this Paul has persuaded and turned away much people, saying that they are not gods, which are made with hands."

He continues on to say this in Verse 27:

"So that not only our craft is in danger to be set at naught; but also that the temple of the great goddess Diana should be despised, and her magnificence should be destroyed, whom all Asia and the world worship."

Demetrius indicated his benefits in the whole affair in Verse 25.

"Sirs, you know that by this craft we have our wealth."

Paul in the book of Romans 1:25 said this about the Roman church;

"Because that, even though they knew God, they glorified him not as God, neither were thankful; but became vain in their imaginations, and their foolish heart was darkened. Professing themselves to be wise, they became fools, and changed the glory of the incorruptible God into an image made like to corruptible man, and to birds, and four-footed beasts, and creeping things."

Thus the Bible in the book of Psalms 115:3-8 says;

"Their idols are silver and gold, the work of men's hands. They have mouths, but they do not speak; eyes they have, but they do not see; they have ears, but they do not hear; noses they have, but they do not smell; they have hands, but they do not handle; feet they have, but they do not walk; nor do they mutter through their throat. Those who make them are like them; so is everyone who trusts in them."

It just beats me why people would prefer to worship things made by man, or believe that man can solve their problems when such people who claim to be

capable of solving others' problems cannot solve theirs.
The book of Hosea 4:10 says;

"They consult a wooden idol and are answered by a stick of wood."

What a pathetic situation, but blessed is the nation whose God is Jehovah! This is not only something that affects the illiterates; it is prevalent across the varying ranks of professions and literacy bands. People en masse worship that which they have created with their own hands. Some worship their human intellect; they worship circular education as god.

With spiritual things, unfortunately, the devil is not intimidated by education or social status of anyone. The fact is, in order for the devil to defeat us as God's children, he needs to have a very sound strategy to do so. The use of his stratagem often implies a concealed intention, and therefore is opposed to a straightforward deal with the intended targets of conning.

The devil through stratagem conceals his true object of spiritual attack. This is in itself comparable to deceit when it is in process, but differs from the classical sense of deceit simply because in the case of his operations, there is no direct breach of any promise with his victims in many and some cases.

The devil, through stratagem simply leaves it to the victims whom he is deceiving to commit the errors of understanding, which at last, flowing into one end result, suddenly change the truth into a lie. Without the revelation knowledge of God, the victims start to make their own interpretations of the Word of God. Do you know that many Christians who live contrary to the word of God genuinely believe that they are on the right track? This truth is also hidden even to the intellectuals who should have the ability to read and comprehend. The victims begin to accept what is wrong for right. This is why God laments in the book of Hosea 4:6 that 'M***y people are dying of ignorance***.'

"Trust in the LORD with all your heart and lean not on your own understanding." (Proverbs 3:5-6)

There are any Christians who are highly religious but are lost into the Devil's lie. To the devil, the dynamics of the human mind in warfare makes the physical destruction of man unnecessary or even unattractive to his operations.

Although to him, in some cases, physical destruction is often a component of defeat; the two are however neither regarded as synonymous nor treated as equal in value. Satan's most frequent and consistent attack is directed against our minds. The devil capitalizes on our ignorance and shortcomings.

God on the other hand does not place any premium on ignorance, and does not pardon on the basis of our plea of ignorance.

"Because that, even though they knew God, they glorified him not as God, neither were thankful; but became vain in their imaginations, and their foolish hearts were darkened." (Romans 1:21)

He assures us that if we know the truth, then only that truth shall set us free. We should seek the truth, so that we are not susceptible and vulnerable to the oxidizing effects of the devil's lies. He that the Son sets free is free indeed!

Satan sends out his hosts with an arsenal of weapons: lies, threats, intimidation, questions, accusations, lusts and other enticements to deny us the fruits of the knowledge of the truth. It is only through his successes in the battle of the mind that physical destruction is guaranteed as a bonus.

Many Christians have fallen to the devil's lies, and truly believe that Satan has got some of influence over their lives, and that he is the cause to all their problems in life. They completely ignore other factors that may have influenced their failures in life. The devil loves this to the bone, and capitalizes on our ignorance and shortcomings; he wants us to believe that he controls our lives.

Because of our natural, human tendency to seek to establish answers to every incident that happens in life, we often assume that causes are similar to their effects, in the same way that important or large effects must have large causes.

When inferring the causes of behavior, we tend to accord too much weight to Satan's influence on the situation, and not so much on the spiritual dispositions of the actor or victim, as well as the situational determinants of the actor's behavior.

People also sometimes overestimate and ignore their own role and blame as both a cause and a target of the behavior of others. Lastly, people often perceive relationships that do not even exist, because they do not even have an intuitive understanding of the kinds and amount of information needed to prove the existence of such a relationship. Many relationships are actually destroyed by perceived things, which are in fact far from reality. The devil operates from within the spheres of these abstracts, and he creates images that are so believable we fall for his trap.

Some Christians even believe that when someone dies, it is because he has sinned against God. Satan often claims to have authority over death. Even though Jesus defeated Satan when he snatched the keys of death, yet his majesty's death and resurrection does not claim to make us immune to 'physical' death. It however gives us the divine hope in the resurrection beyond death.

"Fear not them which kill the body, yet are not able to kill the soul; but rather fear him who is able to destroy both the soul and body in hell."

We may not understand nor comprehend the process of death in the realm of both the saved and the unsaved, but one day we shall understand it in full. Life and death are controlled by God, and him alone. Even his most loved ones will go through death; it is a natural phenomenon. Jesus had to go through the same process too.

Eliphaz the Temanite in the Book of Job 4:7 also insinuated the same when he told Job that nobody who is innocent ever suffers. Job in Job 5:8 responded by saying;

"As for me, I would seek God, and to God I would commit my cause."

The fact is, any mature child of God who listens to the spirit of God would not think of such abstracts, but someone lacking in faith or the knowledge of the Word of God would be susceptible to such absurd and devilish lies.

As humans, we also resist the thought that outcomes can be determined by forces that interact in random and unpredictable ways that are purely coincidental but natural. In my culture and beliefs, lightening strikes are associated with acts of witchcraft, simply because people lack the scientific understanding of the cause of thunder and lightening.

Their believes are reinforced further if someone is actually killed by lightning, and they would attempt to explain what they believe could be the reason why it happened; like being a result of other people being jealous of the deceased's promotion or other achievements in life.

People generally do not accept the notion of chance or randomness in events that take place in life. On our own, we do not have the capacity or the capability to discern such intangibles, and the devil capitalizes on this vacuum.

Traditional witch doctors and psychics also do claim to have the ability to provide reasons to incidents that happen to people's lives, and subsequently provide solutions to the problems. All those who trust in these lies and are enslaved by such absurd beliefs pay exorbitantly. To them, it is simply their means to survival; they also have to pay bills and live decent lives, and so they badly need that money! Their deceptive art is influenced and resourced by the devil himself. Their estimates are based on the field of probabilities.

Successful dice players also often times claim to exert some sort of control or influence over the outcome of a throw of dice, but their assertions are actually a result of probabilities. The same thing applies to traditional witch doctors or psychics; their claims of having answers as well as control over incidents that take place in people's lives, are in fact, deceptive tactics and antics of the devil. It is all outside their control. Their lies are further reinforced especially if certain things turn out the way the witch doctor had predicted.

To provide a more commonsensical approach to this analogy, let me use a common but practical scientific illustration for relativity and easier comprehension. When an object is placed on a surface in an unstable equilibrium, it will presumably fall down. To some people, they will often downplay other factors involved and only blame the fall on the unstable equilibrium.

The fact is, when the object is in unstable equilibrium, it simply means that its centre of gravity is offset. This means that it loses its ability to retain a stable form. The force of gravity acting upon the object outside its centre of gravity will make it to fall. Thus, the instability of the object is the cause, and the effect is its fall through the gravitational pull.

When a systematic analysis of co-variation is not feasible and several alternative causal explanations seem possible, one rule of thumb people use to make judgments of cause and effect is to consider the similarity between attributes of the cause and attributes of the effect. Properties of the cause are then 'inferred on the basis of being correspondent with or similar to properties of the effect.' Heavy things make heavy noises; dainty things move daintily; large animals leave large tracks. When dealing with physical properties, such inferences are generally but not always correct, but spiritual things cannot be explained through such simplistic and shallow reasoning.

The fact is, as humans, we expose ourselves to so much vulnerability that makes us susceptible to spiritual attacks by the devil, and when we fall, we give the credits to the devil for being the sole perpetrator. How many sicknesses and other calamities have been blamed on the devil? Some Christians have even blamed Satan for their breakdown in marriages. Satan may have had a role to play in such situations, but he is not the sole perpetrator. He simply exploits our weaknesses.

We as 'perfect' Christians do not want to appreciate the fact that we also have a role to play in this whole affair. In the book of James 1:14-15, James has this to say.

"One is tempted by one's own desire, being lured and enticed by it; then, when that desire has conceived, it gives birth to sin, and that sin, when it is fully grown, gives birth to death."

We shall delve a little deeper in this scripture so that we take it into perspective and understand it in its totality.

The Bible in the book of Romans 6:23 cautions us that;

"The wages of sin is death, and the gift of God is eternal life."

To many practitioners of spiritual warfare, the first thought that comes to mind in their understanding of the verse is physical death. Death is however a generic expression relating to situations where the 'desired state' ceases to exist; in other circles it is normally understood to be the cessation of all vital phenomena without a potential for instantaneous resuscitation. It can be death in a relationship, financial death, marital death, as well as the premature physical death.

Let me use an example to substantiate my point further. Adultery is a sin before God. A man who indulges in such sin suffers the following types of deaths; he spends the little money that he earns in order to satisfy his multiple partners (resulting in financial death); his relationship with his wife sours and sometimes even dies leading to divorce (marital death); his relationship with God dies (spiritual death); he risks contracting Sexually-Transmitted Infections including Human Immune-deficiency Virus which he would in turn pass on to his wife (could result in premature physical death). These are but a few different types of incapacitations in my examples, which the Bible emphatically refers to as death.

The devil usually starts the psychological attacks very early in peoples' lives, because it is the only way he can assert his influence and build a strong foundation of spiritual bondage through lack of knowledge of the word of God and the truth of his promises. If a child is abused at home, lies from the devil often appear in their thoughts saying the child deserves it or is not worth anything to anyone.

These lies will keep on being re-played and solidified further in their lives as they grow up. As such children are developing and growing up, deceptive questions from the enemy would at times appear in their minds regarding even the true identity and integrity of God, and the veracity of His Word as well as the truth of His divine promises.

Over and over these thoughts emerge, causing confusion, ignominy and fear. Once a child begins to perceive any of such lies as truth, more lies will appear to reinforce the central lies. If there is no intervention by the parents to tell such child the love and mercies of God and His purpose for their lives, after a while the child will begin to focus on his own virtues and shortcomings.

Do we now realize that parenthood is not such an easy task? As parents, we are charged with great responsibilities of not only physically raising up our children, but also to bring them up under the fear and knowledge of God.

Unfortunately, as parents we sometimes ignore such responsibilities, and completely divorce ourselves from the social and spiritual challenges faced by our children, and we would only step in when a child transgresses. As responsible parents, we should know at all times where our children are, with whom they are playing, and the kind of characters that are friends to our children.

Wherever there is lack of responsibility over a child's life by the parents, the devil usually assumes the 'big brother' or 'daddy' role, and would raise up such a child to ultimately serve him. This explains why in societies where it is considered a taboo to even discuss issues of sexuality with children, other older children in the streets will teach your children wrong things concerning sexual conducts.

Such an information-deprived child would instead believe and have confidence in his or her friends, and the parents will only come to realize it when something has gone wrong. Sometimes, such older children who are playing the 'mummy' or 'daddy' or 'big brother' role could be knowingly or unknowingly directed by the devil into such children's lives, to prey on them and add more reinforcements to his lies. The Bible however says;

"It would be better for him if a millstone were put around his neck and he be thrown into the sea than for him to cause one of these little ones to sin." (Luke 17:2)

Furthermore, if parents do not reflect the character of God to their children, the children will project all such shortcomings on to God.

For instance, if one or more parents is cold, lacking in emotion, rigid and constantly preoccupied with other things, is full of hatred and is a spouse or child abuser; then the child will sometimes also see God as lacking compassion, unloving, abusive and not being there for them.

The truth is, the enemy capitalizes on these shortcomings and encourages these perceptions which lead to spiritual bondage later on in their lives.

Many people even bring a lot of bad baggage along with them into adulthood from their childhood. Some grew up in homes where there has been considerable control, manipulation and emotional or physical abuse.

Women are often unobtrusively "led" to find a man of similar qualities to continue the destructive negative reinforcements of the devil's lies in their lives. We cannot underestimate the enemy's influence in these situations.

In many cases, the enemy already has had claims upon parents and even grandparents. Now the enemy focuses on the children, because he knows that the consequences of family sins can make the children vulnerable to similar attacks experienced by their forefathers. This in the medical fraternity would be referred to as *genetically inherited disorders*.

This explains why, people would often assert that marriages of children whose parents have had failed marriages are also bound to fail. It is painful to admit this, but it is true. The devil uses scenes from the parents' marriage and makes it part of the children's married life; if the father was a cheat and wife beater, the devil would tell the daughter that her husband would not be any different from her father.

There is however comforting news to this. Such a chain of spiritual bondage can only be broken through salvation and serious lives of prayer. Unless God builds our marriages, if we try to build it using human intellect, then we do it all in vain. When we come to God, he forgives the sin of our fathers, forefathers, and great forefathers!

"This righteousness from God comes through faith in Jesus Christ to all who believe. There is no difference, for all have sinned and fall short of the glory of God, and are justified freely by his grace through the redemption that came by Jesus Christ. God presented him as a sacrifice of atonement through faith in his blood. He did this to demonstrate his justice, because in his forbearance he forgave the sins committed beforehand - he did it to demonstrate his justice at the present time, so as to be just and the one who justifies those who have faith in Jesus." (Romans 3.22-26)

Often there are strongholds of low self-esteem and self-hatred in children from underprivileged backgrounds. The enemy would capitalize on such shortcomings, and pummel them will lies and accusations, causing much doubt and despondency in their lives. He tells them that they are good-for-nothings, and can never achieve anything substantial in life.

This is the reason why I have, together with some village volunteers, pioneered the NYDRC, which is a youth development and rehabilitation center in the village where I was born and raised. The aim of the center is ensure that children from poor family backgrounds are accorded similar opportunities for faculty development programs similar to their counterparts from wealthier families. We endeavor to teach them the love and purpose of God for their lives so that we lay a strong foundation and inculcate the spirit of self-awareness and appreciation at quite a tender age.

There are some Christians by the number, who have literally resigned themselves to lives of failure. They are destined to defeat by their social circumstances. They will often reside in their comfort zone saying that if my parents, my parents' parents, and my parents' parents' parents (and so on and so forth) were poor, who am I to turn the situation around and live a life of success? But God has not called us to a life of begging; he wants us to be lenders.

Understanding the devil's tactics and strategies can perhaps help in providing a new dimension and perspective on parenthood. Parents are entrusted with children by the Lord to nurture, to cherish and to protect them. In the parent, the child needs to see a reflection of God's attributes of unconditional love, faithfulness and holiness. The parent should also be a steward of God's grace in the home and be on guard against the enemy's assaults on any member of the family.

A godly parent can exercise great authority in the name of Christ to resist the enemy and fight on behalf of the children. Like our Biblical brother Job, a parent is also the priest of the home, bringing the sins of the children to God so that the enemy cannot establish strongholds in their lives.

Back to General Sun Tzu concepts; in his attack strategies he also insisted upon the need to operate against the mind of the enemy-both the enemy commander and his troops. He pointed out that all warfare is based upon deception. Spiritual wars, invariably, are also marred by deceptive tactics planned and executed by Satan himself. The situation prevails even in some churches; everything may outwardly seem to be of God, but may be driven by the devil himself. There are lots of Christians who are drawn in to churches because of the prospects of success or attaining wealth. They simply are miracle-seekers.

"And no wonder! Even Satan disguises himself as an angel of light........."
(2 Corinthians. 11:14-15)

Despite these facts, many of our spiritual warfare teachings tends to completely ignore the aspects of psychology and deception in warfare altogether. The concept of deception is based upon perception. The devil actively feeds the children of God with false information and thoughts in order to mislead them; and the more information and acts of wonders he can feed and display to them, the greater their capacity for being deceived or inundated with irrelevant details.

Sun Tzu's fixation upon the human psychology is ever more relevant today in spiritual warfare than it probably was when he wrote it from a carnal-minded perspective of warfare. At this juncture, and after this very broad survey, I shall now focus more on spiritual warfare applications and I endeavor to depart from the military theories of Sun Tzu and leave that to others who may be interested to study his books and teachings any further, because the scope of his work is far below that of this book, and I intend to just use the principles of warfare as outlined in his book only to illustrate the devil's war-fighting strategies

CHAPTER 5

THE MEANS TO DEFEAT

"Then Saul dressed David in his own tunic. He put a coat of amour on him, and a bronze helmet on his head. David fastened on his sword over the tunic and tried walking."

(1 Samuel 17:38-40)

The real test of a soldier's fighting ability is in war. Warfare as already elucidated, is a clash of ideals and goals; it is a duel on a very extensive scale. It is an act of violence intended to compel our opponents to fulfill our will. War is violent, and the violence is the means; the compulsory submission of the enemy to our will is the ultimate object of war. In the battlefield, targets shoot back, and are not just some non-thinking automatons; they at times think even more than we do.

Spiritual wars are invariably fought in the spiritual theatres and realms by the heavenly hosts. Since war is a clash of ideals and goals, and since it is always the shock of two or more hostile bodies in collision and not the action of a living power upon an inanimate mass; the primary target of the devil then is Christians and not non-Christians because he already has got claims over those who are not saved.

Unfortunately some Christians don't even really want to acknowledge the ugliness of warfare, and spiritual warfare for that matter. They would rather sit in front of a television screen, twiddling their thumbs and just hope the devil would be intimidated or threatened by their passiveness.

War is no pastime; no mere passion for venturing and winning; no work of a simply curious enthusiast; it is a serious means for serious object. All the appearance, which it wears from the varying hues of fortune, all that it assimilates into itself of the oscillations of passion, of courage, of imagination, of enthusiasm, are only properties of the means of war.

It is high time spiritual warfare is also regarded as such, and its challenges regarded as such too. It is more dangerous and challenging than any of the carnal wars that have ever been fought throughout the world history.

No clean warrior ever wins combat. In combat, you just cannot avoid hitting and eating the dirt. In combat, its either you kill your enemy, or he kills you. That's the reality, period.

It does not make any sense then that when it comes to spiritual warfare, Christians would believe that if they act noble, talk nicely, take off their spiritual combat weapons and gear, and present a completely sorry attitude of self-pity before the devil he would not bother them! Unfortunately that is not the devil's character; he is one ruthless contender.

Some Christians actually would prefer to see spiritual combat being fought like a movie footage of a scene from the Gulf War; they want to see devils lashing out from their fighting positions with flares and rockets being fired at them by Christians and a good number of them being killed in the process, and experience extended struggles with sensational endings like at American Holly-Wood or Indian Bolly-Wood, where the main character always wins at the end of the scene.

To them, spiritual combat is a form of a swashbuckling adventure, and they're always the heroes. Their opponent is just an ugly, horned, stupid, non-thinking being who is simply defeated through wish full ideals of combat!

But think of the real guns-and-bombs war: the carnage, death, destruction, and hatred - there are some who find that exciting, though! They need to grasp the truth of how horrible such things really are. Ask any soldier who has experienced actual combat and the rigors of war; death sometimes becomes a vacation well sought after.

Combat builds discipline, enduring spirit, courage, valor, and esprit-de-corps. Through combat, a soldier is accorded the opportunity to put into practice all the skills that he has learned through the art and science of military teachings.

In a study carried out on the impact of combat on soldiers, it was hypothesized that when faced with an impending wartime deployment, soldiers with prior combat experience would report minimal emotional problems accompanied by high rates of level headedness when compared with combat-naive soldiers

"A soldier who can travel a thousand miles without any challenges or problems, travels where the enemy is not situated."

-Sun Tzu

The kind of level headedness that we develop as Christians prepares us for the challenges that we will invariably encounter in our spiritual lives. We develop the right attitude that helps us deal with Satan's attacks very effectively.

However, Satan's work is not at all that simple to discern. It goes on at all sorts of different levels from all sorts of thoughts, people, movements, and happenings.

So, any direct attacks on the work of Satan have their success place, but not always by themselves. A badly aimed attack is like a wrongly prescribed drug that would kill the patient. Ask the sons of Sceva in the book of Acts 19:116. They took spiritual warfare as a joke, and attacked the works of Satan without any ammunition and protection which are only guaranteed through Christ our Lord.

Throughout history, nearly all the world battles which are regarded as the masterpieces of the military art have been battles of maneuver in which very often the enemy has found himself defeated by some novel expedient, or device- some queer, swift, unexpected thrust or stratagem. Strength and muscle power are not the formula, but sheer strategy is.

In such battles the losses of the victors have been small. The Second World War was a classic example. The "Blitzkrieg" strategy, which Hitler and his Nazi regimes employed, was very formidable against the coalition forces. They compensated for their numerical inferiority by avoiding their opponent's strengths and concentrated their efforts on weaknesses, often with tremendous results.

Tactically speaking, German forces lacked the numerical superiority when compared to the coalition forces, but compensated for that deficiency by the application of strategy. Many military analysts today actually believe that Germany could have won the war if it was not because of Hitler's interference with the military plans.

Maneuver strategy is a similar grand war-fighting philosophy that the devil also employs, concerning the means of defeating us through attacking our weaknesses in spiritual combat. It is very quick, violent for a moment, and a very unfair approach.

It is often decisive, even preemptive, at the expense of protocol and posturing of resources because in most cases the aggressor may not have matching resources to his adversary.

Maneuver war-fighting strategy puts greater premium on being sneaky rather than courageous, and it is not at all glorious, because it typically flees from the enemy's strength. In maneuver warfare, strength is not at all too necessary, it is not a formula portion for success, and neither is it a pre-requisite. You employ your strength, regardless of measure, against your opponent's weakness, in order to achieve a big punch with a small fist!

The term maneuver warfare is derived from the parent expression of 'out-maneuvering the opponent'. In his book titled 'The Art of Maneuver', Robert Leonhard points out three distinguishable means of defeat: **preemption**, **dislocation**, and **disruption**. The three terms are not synonymous, even though they have at times been promiscuously inter-changed in usage by non-maneuver practitioners.

In my illustrative use of the three terms, I would like to delve deeper only into the tactical implications of the three innovative approaches to military victory in general terms, and would try to illustrate how each is invariably used by our adversary the devil to achieve victory over the potentially invincible children of the Supreme God.

My wife asked me when she was going through my manuscript, why I say 'potentially' invincible children of the Almighty God. To set this straight, I personally believe that there is no weapon designed by our adversary that can prevail against us. However, this condition is only guaranteed as long as we let Jesus Christ reign supremely in our spiritual lives.

Some people may ask, but why are other Christians from time to time being attacked and seemingly defeated by the devil? This is the reason why I decide to use the term 'potentially.'

Let me take you back to some basic science theories. In the study of physics and matter, an object can store energy as a result of its position. Let us use the following illustration as an example. When a bow is drawn or pulled, it is able to store energy as a result of its position. When assuming its *usual resting position* (i.e., when not drawn), there is no energy stored in the bow. Yet when its position is altered from its usual equilibrium position, the bow is able to store energy by virtue of its position. This stored energy of position is referred to as 'potential' energy. Potential energy is therefore stored energy of position possessed by an object.

When a Christian transgresses, God does not depart from his life. The sin of disobedience forms a chasm between him and God. He will invariably forfeit all the benefits and prophylactic security protection and supplies from God. He is still a child of God, but is not fully exploiting all that which God has intended for him.

He functions like a unit that operates outside the supporting range of its combat support arms; the supporting fires will always fall short of the target!

The same applies to a Christian who trusts his instincts more than the promises of God. Even though he has God on his side, he is using human intellect and carnal measures to fight the spiritual forces. There will finally come a time, when such a Christian gets to the cross-road and he will need some direction and guidance. It is the Spirit of God who guides and directs our spiritual lives. He gives us the strength to overcome any opposition. So, potentially all Christians are invincible, but it is through our own folly and iniquities that we get subjugated by the devil.

The major effort, strategies, and modus operandi of the devil is not geared at the immediate destruction of Christians. As I have alluded before, he very well knows that it would be difficult, if not totally impossible.

So he does not even consider his efforts as being to destroy us, but considers them as simply the means leading to that. The spiritual attacks on the various facets of holy living such as integrity, obedience, fidelity, honesty, sober-mindedness, fear of God, etc, may be the devil's immediate object of battle, but certainly not the ultimate one. In the military teachings, this would be referred to as the ***shaping operations!*** These set conditions that are conducive for the decisive operations or attack.

I wish to hasten to request that the attributes of this description should not be looked upon in any other way less than simply the means of gaining just localized spiritual superiority. Satan desires these conditions just so that at last when he offers the final destructive fight to us, it will be difficult for us to stand against his other wiles.

I have often been asked why I would even discuss the strategies that the devil uses against the children of God, and that I may make him aware of other alternative and effective means of attacking

Christians. I feel the answer to this is very simple. Don't we as Christians think that the devil knows his stuff? Don't we know that he understands and employs tactics and strategies more effectively than the contemporary learned carnal military thinkers? Why would he start to develop a sense of conscious awakening when he either reads or hears me talking about what I have through my experience discerned as being his attack strategies?

He may not call it the way I call it, but it is the application of the war-fighting principles that I would really like us to focus on. And I just hope that this will bring the awareness to Christian brethrens concerning the devil's operations. Have I served in his regiments for me to understand his operations? Again the answer to this is simple. I have earnestly studied his tactics for a very long time now since the day of my salvation. All his schemes are elucidated succinctly in the Word of God, which should be read in order to achieve full understanding of his wiles and deceptive strategies.

CHAPTER 6

PREEMPTION

"David said to the Philistine giant, 'you come to me with a sword, a spear, and a javelin, but I come against you in the name of the Lord almighty, the God of the armies of Israel, whom you have defied. This day the Lord will hand you over to me, and I will strike you down and cut off your head........for the battle is the Lord's.......!'

As the Philistine moved closer to attack him, David quickly ran toward the battle line to meet him.

-1 Samuel 17:45-48

The term preemption is often thought of as pertaining to a strategic-level move that precipitates a war. But the true meaning of the term is much more broader than that. According to the dictionary, it means to buy beforehand, or to circumvent a situation before it crystallizes, seizing an opportunity before the enemy does.

Shaka Zulu king of the Zulus was perhaps one of the greatest African Generals of the late eighteenth century whose use of strategy has always inspired me during my early years as an officer.

As far as the European recognition is concerned, the last glorious achievement of the Zulu army was the battle of *Isandhlawana* on January 22, 1879, where the Zulus, armed with spears and clubs, wiped out a sizeable strength of the British regiment, rendering their high-tech cannons and guns of that time useless against Zulu's war-fighting strategy of swift surprise attacks. Shaka believed that in order to defeat your opponent, you first have to expose his weakness, and then you strike his vital organs to kill him. He demonstrated himself to be of great character capable of innovative thought and decisive action.

However, just like many European commanders of the past who have employed preemption in the past, he is also often ridiculed by military analysts of the contemporary era as having lacked the skill and circumspection because he often attacked his enemies when they were fully unprepared and unsuspecting.

The fact however is, war is not intended to be fair. The devil's tactics are also regarded as being unfair! In warfare, fairness is the expression of those destined and resigned to defeat. It is the defense of the feeble-minded.

A commander who preempts his enemy may be numerically stronger or weaker than his foe; his weapons may be better or worse; his fighting doctrine may be ingenious or poor; but the one assert that he alone posses is resolve. His decisive approach to the impending conflict is not incrementally superior to the enemy but overwhelmingly so. As a result, he earns the scorn of those who evaluate his operations, but he also snatches victory.

Characteristically, the victory is cheap in terms of human life. The devil is very relentless in pursuit of victory, and this is the one asset that he possesses. Unfortunately, some spiritual warfare practitioners would only attack the devil as and when they see certain indicators of his operations, and would not circumvent the situation even before it is manifest.

We should be proactive rather than reactive, so that we can deny him the freedom of operation in terms of initiative. This is why God tells us to shod our feet with sandals in preparation for the gospel of peace, so that the devil does not wrest the initiative from us through his lies.

The devil does not posses any greater spiritual might, and he is very much aware that he cannot stand up and fight God and His children in a clean and fair fight. He therefore prefers to attack the church of Jesus Christ using deceptive preemptive tactics, when they are least expecting his offensives or are not spiritually prepared. He waits for opportunities in a Christian's life when there is a degradation in spiritual well being (to include prayer life), before he can attempt to snatch that quick victory.

The Bible in 1 Peter 5:8 equates Satan's tactics to that of a roaring lion roaming about, waiting for someone to devour.

"Be sober and self-controlled. Be watchful. Your adversary the devil, walks around like a roaring lion, seeking whom he may devour."

We should endeavor to examine deeper the true implications of such analogy and comparisons. Understanding the characteristics and hunting strategies of lions could perhaps help the spiritual warriors understand why God simply equates the devil's tactics and prowess to that of a lion.

In Africa, the African lions are much bigger and more aggressive than the European mountain lions, and are the most feared of the predator species; but lions become man-eaters less often than tigers, but when they do they are bolder and more aggressive in their pursuit of human meat. A man-eating lion often hunts at night and prowls the perimeter of villages looking for victims to devour.

A lion is however not the swiftest animal in the animal kingdom; neither does it have the enduring spirit like other predators. It simply relies upon preempting its prey whilst they are relaxed, either feeding or drinking water. Lions are not particularly efficient and skilled hunters. They can successfully capture their prey, which consist of medium-sized ungulates including zebras, wildebeests and antelope in only 20 to 30 percent of their attempts. They are referred to as "opportunistic" hunters, eating whatever they can catch for themselves or steal from other predators. They are not well adapted for leaping or reaching particularly high speeds, nor are they capable of running for long distances. In short, if the lion is not successful within a few hundred meters, they give up the chase and the prey escapes.

"Resist the devil, and he shall flee." (James 4:7)

This is quite comforting to know that our adversary the devil also lacks the enduring spirit; so constantly resist his attempts, and he shall flee! The devil is however not threatened by any nice talking, good mannered fighter; you need to tell him off straight on that you don't want anything to do with him and his lies. He needs to get it right, otherwise he will loiter around hoping for a change of heart.

Two important causes of hunting failures of lions is a result of the fault in the actual stalking of the prey and in the execution of their famous lion charge. Lions do not hunt by scent, although their sense of smell is excellent; they often approach prey from an upwind location thereby alerting the prey and ending the hunt. Secondly, the lion's charge is generally launched directly at its quarry and it rarely alters the path of the attack, as do other predators.

Generally speaking, if a lion misses it's quarry on the initial charge, it does not give pursuit, but quits and looks for new quarry. Field observations reveal that lions spend a great deal of time looking for circling vultures and listening for the calls of hyenas, enabling them to locate downed prey. When prey and other predators are plentiful, lions may get close to half of their food by scavenging. They would fight over the carrion with other predators such as hyenas without any shame.

The Bible also equates the devils tactics to that of a thief who steals by night when the owners are sleeping.

The primary strength that thieves rely on is stealth, as well as exploiting weaknesses in security. There is a very good reason why the Bible does not refer to Satan as a robber!

In the military applications of nighttime operations, there are abounding advantages of night attacks. The advantages are increased when your opponent is not trained and equipped for night operations. At night, everybody rests from the toils of the day, there is less security, and the reaction is thus slower. A good night attack is reliant upon the speed in execution. The factors that govern the decision to launch a night attack are either to compensate for paucity in resources, or to functionally deny your opponent the ability to bring his military might to bear.

Military night operations call for disciplined, nonchalant, self-reliant troops. The mental strain involved in night combat is severe; it is easier to endure combat stress in periods of activity than during long spells of inactivity. This is why at night-even more so than by day-he who takes the initiative has the advantage. However, since orientation and co-ordination will become increasingly difficult, this initial advantage diminishes as the attack progresses.

Darkness is helpful in achieving tactical surprise, and the attacker will derive additional advantages from the defender's inability to aim his weapons effectively. Nights are normally used for resting, and for this reason fatigue and symptoms of exhaustion afflict those who have to stay awake. Imagine how unprepared for reaction you would be if you were to be attacked in the middle of your deep sleep!

The Biblical implications of nighttime, however, refer to the dark times of a Christian's spiritual life. It can be the time when a child of God is facing great spiritual challenges, a death in the family, a death in marriage or relationships, and maybe a death in their financial well being. Satan is an opportunist, and he attacks us during our night times.

The devil is also referred to as being sly like a snake. Snakes kill their prey by preemptive strikes. They attack before the prey makes an effective move. Preemption, consequently, often eschews what is normally considered proper tactical dispensation.

Indeed, the idea of preemption includes a rejection- whether implied or stated; of established fighting methods. Shaka Zulu introduced the short-stabbing spear or *assegai* against the throwing spears of his opponents. This clearly portrayed his fighting tactics as being unfair as he would wait for his opponents to expend their spears whereupon he would close up and destroy them in close combat.

David began his fight against the Philistine by refusing to don on Saul's body amour. Then he ran toward Goliath rather than stalking him, just as a unit employing preemption would move in column formation for the sake of speed rather than in line or even echelon for the sake of security.

Goliath completely expected a fair fight; that is David coming towards him, starting up a fight in a more gentlemanly fashion, and the outcome of the battle being decided by the physically stronger fighter with greater muscle throwing power and yielding weapons with greater mass, speed and lethality.

Before he had exerted a lot of energy scuffling with the seemingly immovable giant, and risking sustaining injuries during the scuffle, David's opponent was already fallen and submitted before the fight was started.

American 'Iron' Mike Tyson's fights were also characterized by the principles of preemption. He would overwhelm his opponent with heavy blinding punches and before his opponent recollected his composure, he would be down and knocked out through his famous upper-cut punch. His victories were achieved within the first rounds of the bout. He may not have known it or even called it pre-emption; just as a snake employing preemptive strikes would not know that it is employing preemption!

It is often characteristic of preemptive moves that they often obviate battles. For example, when Joshua attacked the city, he was given a grandeur plan as to how he should execute his offensive actions. He did not apply carnal measures, and completely discarded the counsel of military common sense. The military teachings prescribe that an attacking force should not make any noise when advancing to contact with the enemy if it wants to achieve a surprise attack with some decisive results. The attacking force would utilize geographically covered and concealed routes to the attack position, and deny the defender to employ their direct and /or indirect fires before the assault line or line of contact.

Joshua threw such teachings to the winds and sang praises to God as he was moving around the city seven times. Such a move can also be classified as preemptive, because it fulfils several important criteria. First it set aside conventional caution. Secondly, though it depended on the power of God through the singing rather than on carnal weapons, its primary objective was to dislodge the enemies within the city before they could fight.

CHAPTER 7

DISLOCATION

"Reaching into his bag and taking out a stone, he slung it and struck the Philistine on the forehead. The stone sank into his forehead, and he fell face down on to the ground."

-1 Samuel 17:49

Dislocation is the art of rendering the enemy's strengths irrelevant to the fight. Instead of having to fight or confront Christians on their terms, the devil avoids any combat in which a Christian can bring his full spiritual authority to bear.

A spiritual warrior must bring discipline to his spiritual life and to his actions so that he denies the devil the spiritual advantage. If he allows these areas to be compromised, he will not be effective in resisting the enemy. He should also take sin very seriously, because sin always gives the adversary a spiritual advantage. He must always be on guard against comparing himself with others and being entrapped by the subtlety of religious pride.

The true warrior knows that he can do nothing that is effective with his own strength. His strength, authority, wisdom and discernment are dependent upon his close walk with the Lord. He should always remain focused and guard himself against distraction caused by problems and troubles that appear in his life.

These distractions are designed by the devil to get his eyes off the Lord and lure him into his killing grounds. The spiritual warrior would then start to work and walk in the flesh. This will invariably functionally dislocate the spiritual warrior and misdirect his efforts, thus denying him ability to fully bring his spiritual authority to bear.

A true warrior has the assurance that even though a thousand can fall near him, and ten thousands by his side; the effects of the devil's lashes shall not come even near him, because he has made the Lord his God; he has made Him his habitation!

"He who dwells in the shelter of the Most High will rest in the shadow of the Almighty. I will say of the LORD, "He is my refuge and my fortress, my God, in whom I trust." Surely he will save you from the fowler's snare and from the deadly pestilence." (Psalms 91)

The most common strategy that the devil employs in rendering Christians' strengths irrelevant to the fight is to remove them from the source of their strengths, or conversely remove the source of their strengths away from them. This could be related to their personal walk with God, strengths within the church structure, or other areas of their lives.

Christians fight spiritual warfare on daily basis. This invariably includes even our work places. Christians often would wonder, when they pray for certain burdens in their lives, the devil would instead attack them on things that they had not established as prayer items.

There is a true story of a certain charismatic church in the United States. The spirit of God was really moving, and God reigned supremely in the members' lives. Many people were being saved by the numbers.

The church then decided to spice up the services by hiring another pastor from a different denomination to lead the church. They wanted a more academically-achieved pastor, someone who was about knowledgeable on current affairs. They wanted a more accommodating pastor, someone who could adapt to global social changes and make adjustments in God's plan and principles in order to suit and match the contemporary spiritual challenges.

The new pastor was exactly that, and quite different from the old pastor in many respects. The first time he took the pulpit, he literally tore up the congregation with very well-articulated sermons.

Furthermore, he also instituted many changes in the conduct of affairs in the church. He devoted much of the service time to singing, and lesser time for the preaching of the word. The Bible studies were characterized by debate sessions, people approached the things of God through the carnal mind, thus adulterating it and changing it into the devil's lie. Sometimes the pastor would even start and finish his short sermon without having prayed.

The result; many Christians just gave up the good fight of faith, and many backslid. It became a confused state of affairs. Ultimately, the whole ministry just collapsed, because God was no longer in command.

I write all these to say this; that even though the change of pastors was viewed by other Christians as a new positive development, consultation with God was never made. It was not a move decided by God.

The devil knew that in order for him to bring his little strength to bear, he had to start off by removing the source of strength from the church, or the church from the source of its strength. As a result, the church became leaderless because God was no longer in control, and the strengths of the church members were rendered irrelevant and useless against the attacks of the adversary.

Sun Tzu in his teachings states that '**an army of deer led by a lion is more feared and likely to win than an army of lions led by a deer.**'

"If God is for us, then who can be against us?" (Rom. 8:31-32)

The Bible does not call for righteous Christians, but rather subservient Christians. We are not saved by our deeds, but by the grace of our Lord Jesus, which endures forever, Amen! It did not matter whether the new pastor had the highest circular honors, or his church could generate enough funds to buy the entire world, or the church could heal all kinds of ailments; if Jesus was not the founder and King in that church there was no way possible that it would survive the wiles of the adversary.

"Unless God builds a house, he who builds it does so in vain, and unless God watches over a house, he who watches over it spends the whole night in vain." (Psalms 127)

In our Biblical text example, David employed dislocation in order to negate Goliath's strengths. Goliath never had a chance to throw his spear; he never swung his spear, and never used his shield. Those factors, upon which Goliath's fighting doctrine depended-were never permitted in the conflict. David in 1 Samuel 17:45-46 hinted his intentions when he shouted;

"You come against me with a sword, a spear, and a javelin; but I come against you in the name of the Lord Almighty!"

There are two great prepositions in David's statement: Goliath approaches the fight ***with*** carnal might, but David comes to it ***in*** the name of the Lord**.** That is, David's perspective on the impending battle was altogether different from Goliath's. He did not try to match Goliath's carnal strengths ***with*** carnal strength as his opponent did. Instead, he used his sling ***in*** the name of the Almighty God, to functionally dislocate; that is to render irrelevant, the Philistine's great weapons and strengths.

Someone may argue, how really relevant is the incident when we know that God obviously fought for David!? My point is, it is now possible and easier to make such assessments as to whether God was on David's side or not.

It does not take a figurative rocket scientist to figure out the relative strengths of the two fighters; Goliath was potentially invincible, and David had lesser physical strengths than his opponent. It was a complete mismatch; imagine Mike Tyson being paired with a skinny teenager in a boxing match!

The fighter who was to win such a duel needed ingenious strategy, and in this case it was David who did not implore his limited carnal wisdom to fight Goliath. God gave him the wisdom, and he employed it against Goliath's seemingly superior and invincible strengths.

The bottom line is Christians are potentially invincible as I have already alluded. The only time that the devil can defeat us is by attacking our weaknesses. I am not talking about natural and situational weaknesses. When we start to work on our own and do not let God take charge of our lives, we automatically start to exhibit spiritual weaknesses. The devil invariably attacks such to defeat us.

"He is conceited, knowing nothing, but obsessed with arguments, disputes, and word battles, from which come envy, strife, and reviling, evil suspicions." (1Timothy 6:4)

"The fear of the LORD is the beginning of knowledge: but fools despise wisdom and instruction." (Proverbs 1:7)

As maneuver theory absolutely demands the avoidance of enemy strength, the devil also craftily fights along these lines in terms of functionally rendering irrelevant, rather than facing us in our spiritual strengths. By fighting on our own we simply approach the spiritual fight from the same angle Goliath approached his fight against David, and the end to this all is shameful defeat on us by the devil.

CHAPTER 8

DISRUPTION

"When the Philistines saw that their hero was dead, they turned and ran away. Then the men of Israel and Judah surged forward with a shout and pursued the Philistines."

-1 Samuel 17:51-52

Disruption is the art of defeating the enemy by attacking his Center of Gravity. The Centre of Gravity or CoG as a military concept was developed by a Prussian military theorist by the name of Carl von Clausewitz. The definition of CoG, according to the United States Department of Defense is "those characteristics, capabilities, or locations from which a military force derives its freedom of action, physical strength, or will to fight."

Thus, the Center of Gravity is usually seen as the "source of strength". Accordingly, the Army tends to look for a single center of gravity, normally in the principal capability that stands in the way of the accomplishment of its own mission.

In short, the US Army considers a "friendly" CoG as that element-a characteristic, capability, or locality-that enables one's own or allied forces to accomplish their objectives. Conversely, an opponent's CoG is that element that prevents friendly forces from accomplishing their objectives.

On the contrary, some schools of thought actually define CoG as being your most critical vulnerability. I concur with the latter, because the Center of Gravity is that aspect of your opponent, which when attacked or neutralized would lead to either a temporary or permanent paralysis to his overall fighting capacity. This is likened to a kick in the groin, a punch on the solar plexus! As a fighter, a kick on my solar plexus can result in either temporary or permanent paralysis of my fighting capacity. On the contrary, I don't think that I derive my physical strength from my solar plexus or my most vital organs; they simply are my critical vulnerabilities or my Centre of Gravity which needs to be greatly protected.

In the spiritual analogy, the source from where I derive my spiritual authority and strength is Christ. Any attack on this source will be absolutely suicidal to the devil, and he very well knows this. What then does he do? He simply removes the source of my strength from me because he cannot remove the source of my strength from me.

The devil therefore creates spiritual weaknesses in our lives. Spiritual weaknesses appear in our lives as sin, which we contend with every day of our spiritual lives. With sin comes anger, irritability, exasperation, depression, discouragement, melancholy, despondency, gloominess, bitterness, hatred, resentment, self-pity, hopelessness, despair, paranoia, envy, jealousy, family conflict, arguing, divorce, drunkenness or other addictions, and competitiveness as self-centeredness deepens. These are our critical vulnerabilities which the devil invariably exploits.

"When Jesus spoke again to the people, he said, "I am the light of the world. Whoever follows me will never walk in darkness, but will have the light of life." (John 8:12)

We should at all times protect our critical vulnerabilities so that we deny the devil the opportunity to exploit them.

Consider the following examples of 'critical vulnerability' concept if you are still tactically lost. If you have a bee nest in your house, how would you get rid of the killer insects? To a non tactician, the quick answer would be to kill the bees through incremental attrition. This is a shallow way of dealing with a very complex situation. There is a major difference between defeat and destroy, which as I have said before, the devils knows very clearly the difference between the two and he does not confuse them.

A more prudent way of dealing with this situation would be to first identify the Center of Gravity of the bee colony. The strengths of the colony are the worker or soldier bees, but the critical vulnerability is the queen. Simply kill the queen, and the colony goes away. Thus there would be no further requirement to annihilate the entire bee colony. Do vice versa, and you will spend the rest of your life till fighting the colony with great loss of lives on your part.

This is however easier said than done. The enemy would heavily protect his Center of Gravity. Even Satan knew very well that he could not directly attack Job; he would not have achieved anything substantial. In the book of Job 1:10, he says this to God;

"Then Satan answered the LORD, and said, does Job fear God or not? Have you not made a hedge around him, and about his house, and about all that he has on every side? You have blessed the work of his hands, and his substance is increased in the land."

The fact is, in order to attack the enemy's critical vulnerability, you would have to sequence your attack plan and deliver your effort through a series of shaping efforts.

To defeat the bee colony, you start off by sprinkling some insecticide granules covered with sweet paste on the hive. The worker bees, thinking it is food would then carry it to the queen bee, which upon ingesting it would die. Once the queen is dead, the rest of the bee colony would go away. If you kill the queen, it does not matter how many worker bees or drones you get. The masses are irrelevant to the campaign.

The aim of disruption, then, is to avoid having to physically destroy the entire physical component of the opposing forces through direct attack and incremental attrition, in favor of rendering it inert by discerning and attacking its critical vulnerability only.

There is a Bible verse in Isaiah 59:19 that says;

"When the enemy comes sweeping like a flood, the spirit of the Lord raises the standards against him."

Pastor Benny Hinn in his book titled '**Good Morning Holy Spirit**' points out that in the original Hebrew version there is not much punctuation as is found in the English literature, and claims that the passage actually reads;

"When the enemy comes, then sweeping like a flood, the spirit of the Lord raises the standard against him!"

He insists that it is the Spirit of God that comes sweeping like a flood, thus raising the standards at which the battle is waged, and subsequently submerging all our spiritual opposition. I am obviously not a Hebrew scholar myself, but I find this more comforting than the credits and accolades that we give to the devil about the spiritual strengths that he does not possess.

The fact is, in the first reading version, the devil seems to possess great spiritual strengths. The devil however cannot afford any battle where he is forced to attack the church of the Almighty God on a wide front, but rather he identifies a weakness or critical vulnerability, and concentrates overwhelming spiritual attack at a point of decision in order to bring about a momentary defeat.

In our Biblical text example, the critical vulnerability of the army of Philistia was Goliath. He was the model of the Philistia army; he was the self-imposed leader by virtue of his unmatched physical strength. He was the source from where they derived their moral courage. He was the reason for their courage; in fact, he was their courage. Once David destroyed the giant, there was no further evidence of cohesion among the Philistines. They fled immediately and were pursued by the victorious Israelites. Thus there was no need for a battle in which hundreds, or perhaps thousands, might have perished on both sides.

David did not gain victory over the Philistines through incremental attrition of the entire physical component of the enemy force. He became a champion in one day by simply destroying the Philistine army's Center of Gravity, or critical vulnerability.

"Saul has killed his thousands and David his ten thousands." (1 Sam. 18:7)

Another circular example could be derived from the American 'Iron' Mike Tyson's boxing career. Mike

Tyson was, and is undoubtedly the strongest boxer the world has ever known. His strengths were his courage, and his ability to deliver deadly and bone-crunching upper-cut blows. He may have lacked skill as compared to the likes of Muhammad Ali, but such was compensated for by his great physical strengths. His Center of Gravity, or critical vulnerability, however was stamina and lack of fighting skill. He made sure that all his kills were done within the first rounds of the bout.

Invincible as he was, he was however defeated during his boxing career. The boxers that ever defeated him were not physically robust and aggressive as he was, but the one thing that they had which he lacked was dexterity. They studied all his fights and discovered that his critical vulnerability was stamina and lack of skill. To directly attack him when he was still fit would have been like a stupid dog that runs directly onto the porcupine's quills.

They therefore exposed his vulnerabilities by prolonging the fight to seven or eight rounds, and when his Centre of Gravity was exposed, they pitted overwhelming punches against that condition and achieved the victory. Ask Lenox Lewis and Buster Douglas how they did it!

Just like in any form of combat, by directly pitting your strength against your enemy's strength is very costly in terms of human losses. In our case, the devil would suffer great losses with absolutely no losses on God's side. Just as water runs off hard rock surfaces, and moves in through cracks to destroy a big mountain, the devil also avoids our strengths and attacks our weaknesses in order to defeat us.

The fact is, in some churches the critical vulnerability is the church leadership itself. The members are simply children who do not wean off breast milk and their growth remains stagnant throughout their lives. They cannot think on their own without the church leadership; they can not even fight any situations simply because they rely on the pastor to tell them at all times what weapon system to use, what engagement ranges to set on the sights, and how to 'duck' incoming enemy arrows.

The pastor is not God, and he too is fighting the battle from his end; unless of course he is superman. In this scenario, there is very little that the devil has to do in order to defeat such a church; all he simply does is to destroy the leadership and the entire church collapses!

Thus Sun Tzu also observed that **'To win one hundred battles in one hundred wars is not the acme of skill; but to subdue your enemy without fighting is the supreme excellence'.**

More than in any form of maneuver, disruption capitalizes upon the intangibles of war; psychology, surprise, vulnerabilities and fear. It holds very little respect for quantifiable estimates of the enemy, because it recognizes that above all, an army is made up of human souls. In my earlier example, I pointed out that it really does not matter how much the church cost, and the level of education of the members; the devil places no premium on education, and he deceives the educated on things, which are seemingly plain even to the illiterates.

David was a small boy in stature, and in fact quite a lot of the Israelites, including his own brothers, despised and undermined his fighting prowess. Goliath, on the other hand, was the most hideous, most ugly, most arrogant, most pompous giant that ever breathed life. He was naturally well built, and his pose was very much intimidating. Unfortunately, in warfare and warfare it was, his size did not guarantee him a win. The good fight of faith in David was the determinant in the fight.

'It is not the size of the dog in the fight that matters, but rather the fight in the dog which is a determinant.'

Disruption insists that an army is defeated not when its weapons are destroyed or its armor pierced, but rather when its will to continue the fight is lost. Spiritual wars are also invariably won and lost in the minds and souls of man.

The Bible encourages us to habitually pray in the spirit, because it is in the human soul and spirit that battles are easily lost. The book of Ephesians 6:18 says;

"And pray in the Spirit on all occasions with all kinds of prayers and requests. With this in mind, be alert and always keep on praying for all the saints."

History abounds with examples of armies that had suffered terribly in battles and campaigns and yet retained their fighting spirit and effectiveness. Likewise, there is a an example of Job in the Bible, who even though he was disfigured beyond recognition by a disease more deadly than the highly talked about AIDS; when he was forsaken by not only his friends, but also his wife; he persevered and ultimately won the spiritual campaign.

"But as for me, I know that my Vindicator lives, and that He will at last stand forth upon the dust; and from my flesh I shall see God; my inmost being is consumed with longing. Whom I myself shall see: my own eyes, not another's, shall behold him." (Job 19)

The enduring spirit is evident in the above text; an attack on his health did not metamorphose into a defeat. His will to continue holding on was inspired by the fact that he knew that his redeemer, God, was alive and that he would one day receive his justice.

The devil is a master tactician; in fact, military tactics are either influenced by him or by God! He possesses the most efficient information collection capabilities that surpass modern acquisition systems.

'I have just been to the world, moving to and fro......' (Job 1:7)

Even though he moves about aimlessly, his mission is with the aim of identifying weaknesses in our spiritual lives. Such weaknesses may be in our prayer lives, behavioral problems such as bad temperament, deceit, malice, sexual infidelity, tale bearing, laziness, or it can be social problems in the family, finances, and health. Once he identifies the weakness, he then uses the little strength he has and creates rapture in our lives. Once he has done that, he brings in other powerful forces of darkness, and would slowly destroy all the components that make up an upright Christian.

Let us look at another true story of how the devil sequentially and systematically attacks through a series of decisive points, thus creating weaknesses that would then set the desired conditions which are conducive to the attack on our critical vulnerabilities.

Thomas, or Tom, as he was affectionately called, was a born again, spirit-filled child of God. He worked for a larger corporation in the busiest part of the downtown area in the city of Gaborone. He had such a wonderful relationship with God, and everything he did brought nothing but glory to God.

At work, his secretary Susie was a happy-go-lucky, devil-may-care brand of a person. She lived every day of her life to the fullest. She was a very beautiful young lady; single, intelligent, friendly, and quite almost everything a man would want in a woman.

Susie was however not saved, and her moral convictions were based more on human convictions and not the principles of God.

One good day Susie invited Tom for dinner at her plush apartment in the outskirts of the town. Tom agreed. As they were seated across each other at the dinner table, Tom saw beyond Susie not death, but a mind-wrecking wonderful erotic experience. He made his advances. The good old, ever gentle, Spirit of God whispered to him that;

"For the wages of sin is death, but the free gift of God is eternal life in Christ Jesus our Lord." (Romans 6:23).

As he hesitated, the opposing devil told him that 'King David had sex with Bathsheba the wife of Uriah the Hittite, but is still considered even today as the greatest man ever after God's own heart!'

Tom thought, surely a one off experience would not cost him his life. He would repent afterwards, and again nobody would know about his little escapade.

The spirit of God cautioned him that;

"He who conceals his sins will not prosper, but he who confesses and forsakes them will obtain mercy." (Proverbs 28:13)

The devil employed reverse psychology and threw in another scripture to him that;

"If you confess your sins, God is faithful and just to forgive and cleanse you of all unrighteousness." (I John 1:9)

Tom assured himself that surely this would be just a one-day thing; he would not repeat it again. It is a very small sin anyway, his is better than that of other Christians who kill or flirt with other people's spouses! So this has got to be simply a 'venial' sin!

The world dictionary defines a venial sin as a sin easily excusable or forgiven. It's a relatively unimportant, small sin — not that big a deal. Everybody does it. You can't avoid doing it. It won't really destroy you. The Bible rejects that theory. There is no such thing as an easily excusable or easily forgiven sin. There is no such thing as a little sin if in fact we infer that its effects are little.

There is no such thing as a small sin if we infer that it has no real danger connected with it and does no damage to the perpetrator. No sin is so little that, by itself, it will not condemn the perpetrator to death. This is what the devil wanted Tom to believe, so that he could establish his foothold, and subsequently launch other attacks on his spiritual life. Ultimately, Tom gave in to the devil's lie. He and Susie ended up doing what he knew he was not supposed to do.

That single night experience cost Tom dearly, and adversely affected his spiritual life. Thereafter, every time he tried to pray, the devil would turn on the video recordings of the incident, and would tell Tom that there was no way a Holy God would listen to the prayers of a fornicator. As his prayer life got affected, he ceased to associate with other children of God. He would even ignore to answer his cellular phone whenever his pastor tried to call him.

He began to see of Susie more and more everyday. Nightclubs replaced the church, and beer drinking substituted for being inebriated in the spirit. Speaking in tongues was replaced by speaking in profane tongues. The fire within him died, and was replaced by smoke from cigarettes.

"And therefore God gave them over in the sinful desires of their hearts to sexual impurity for the degrading of their......... They exchanged the truth of God for a lie......" (Rom. 1:24-25)

A visit to Tom after two years found him now living in a small, rented one-roomed house in the poor part of town. He had sold his Mercedes Benz E320 sedan, and had lost his good job due to absenteeism and poor service delivery. As if this was not enough,

Susie had walked out on him, leaving him with the dreaded HIV virus.

"But among you there must not be even a hint of sexual immorality, or of any kind of impurity, or of greed, because these are improper for God's holy people." (Ephesians 5:3)

The story about Tom may seem out of place and a very crude example to some critics, but the moral behind it serves to demonstrate just how the devil systematically and sequentially destroys the lives of upright children of God. The sin of sexual immorality is the main effort of the devil's spiritual attack plan inside as well as outside the church. The New Testament church talks vehemently against this great sin.

Satan and his hosts know beyond a shadow of a doubt that in order to destroy other facets of an upright spiritual Christian, and even non-Christians for that matter; he has to attack our critical vulnerabilities. They work very hard to draw men and women into sexual sins and perversions because it is a direct attack on the only institution that God established before the fall of Adam and Eve at the Garden of Eden.

I'm talking about marriage. God created mankind in his own image (Gen. 1:27). After he had created Adam and put him in the Garden of Eden, the Lord said;

"It is not good for the man to be alone. I will make a helper suitable for him." (Gen. 2:18).

"For this reason a man will leave his father and mother and be united to his wife, and they will become one flesh." (Gen. 2:24)

Today, there are those who are trying to redefine marriage by spicing it up with Satan's recipes. The most common but powerful tool that Satan uses to destroy the fabric, the firebrand of our society is an attack on the institution of marriage. Many Christians unfortunately are completely oblivious of this scheme of the devil.

There is infidelity amongst married couples; Christians and non-Christians. Some justify their actions by saying that it helps to strengthen the marriage. They say that one needs to change their 'sexual' diet daily, and not eat the same type of food all the time, everyday.

This is the worst of absurdity, it is devoid of even scientific reasoning; in fact it is intellectually bankrupt. It is the scheme of deception that Satan employs in order to completely annihilate the children of God.

Marriage, as God has ordained it, is the foundation of a family and families are the foundation of society. When marriages are destroyed, families are also destroyed severely, and the society eventually is affected in an adverse way.

This is all part of Satan's master plan to divide and conquer. He penetrates weaknesses in relationships, and such weakness may be created by one party denying the other their conjugal rights. The disadvantaged partner usually attempts to justify their infidelity by claiming sexual deprivation.

On the other side of the coin, anyone who knowingly manipulates or denies his/her partner their conjugal rights is working against God's instructions for a healthy relationship.

"The husband should give his wife her conjugal rights, and likewise the wife to her husband......Do not deprive one another except perhaps by agreement for a set time; to devote yourself to prayer, and then come together again, so that Satan may not tempt you because of your lack of self-control." (1 Corinthians. 7:3-5)

The devil exploits our lack of self-control, which usually results in adultery. We create opportunities in our marriages by denying our spouses their conjugal rights without any sensible reason. God knows what makes us vulnerable to the devil's temptations, and has recommended this as the formula portion for health in marriage, and failure to observe such divine advice is the cause to many sexual sins committed even in the church.

I wish to hasten to disclaim any impression of attempting to justify this, but all I am insinuating is that in as much as the perpetrator is not justified before God for indulging in adultery, the spouse who denies his/her partner their sexual rights without any recourse works against that which God has warned us against.

"He who scorns instruction will pay for it, but he who respects a command is rewarded. The teaching of the wise is a fountain of life, turning a man from the snares of death. Good understanding wins favor, but the way of the unfaithful is hard." (Proverbs 13:13-15)

One thing that should be absolutely clear is that whenever we do things contrary to the word of God, then we are really acting in disobedience. Why is it that we (including Christians) pay heed to what our circular doctors tell us is right or wrong for our health; we pay particular attention to whatever we eat, and so on and so forth. Why then when God tells us that denying our spouses their conjugal rights will make us vulnerable to the snares of the devil, we take Him for a joke? Don't we know that He knows better the consequences of such attitude?

You cannot manipulate and hold your spouse at ransom by denying them their rights, where exactly do you expect them to gratify their desires? If you do not have any sexual feelings, probably it is best you just do not commit to anyone in marriage. I know this will spark a lot of resentment amongst the readers, especially those who are trying to assist God in re-defining marriage.

"The wise woman builds her house, but the foolish tears it down with her own hands." (Proverbs 14)

All these said, sexual immorality is still an unjustifiable sin, regardless of who you are doing it with or your reasons for committing it.

"Do you not know that he who unites himself with a prostitute is one with her in body? For it is said, 'The two will become one flesh."

(1 Corinthians 6:16)

This sounds very cruel of our God. Imagine becoming one flesh with someone through sexual sin and that person is already in bondage and dealing with a lot of spiritual challenges. I know of a lot of people who were attacked by the same satanic spirits that were afflicting their sexual partners.

There are very powerful spiritual forces, which usually attack both parties to the sexual crime, and this is so because the Bible says that since you are now "one flesh," you are vulnerable to sharing in the bondage of that person, and are susceptible to any form of spiritual attacks that the devil launches on that person. We see the result of this continuously in people's lives. God simply permits it to happen. When a believer continues in sexual sin, this is a definite act of rebellion in an attempt to gratify oneself sexually and emotionally.

"The evil deeds of a wicked man ensnare him; the cords of his sin hold him fast." (Proverbs 5:22)

Unfortunately, there are other "one flesh" bonds acquired through rape, incest and molestation. No wonder the effects of these terrible experiences do not ever seem to let go even after very intense counseling programs, especially if there is no intervention through intercession. There is more than just psychological damage inflicted upon the victims of such crimes. There is also a spiritual hold that compounds the psychological problems. There is bondage in place that needs God's deliverance.

It does not suffice to administer just psychiatric counseling to the victim; spiritual counseling is the lasting remedy. How many rape victims have committed suicide even after a seemingly successful psychiatric counseling? This is because we tend to address issues on the surface, and ignore the subcutaneous structures that will in the process manifest as the real problem.

I very much am supportive of medical science, but I believe that it needs to be complemented with other remedies in order to achieve complete cure of social problems. The authority we have in Jesus' name is however a complete regimen for the healing process.

This is the real unknown reason why suicide is a very complex issue to solve; it is because we are attacking the shadow, and not the object. Why do you think that even psychiatrists tend to link certain moral decays such as murder, serial killings, rape, incest, pedophilia, and stealing, on the past childhood experiences of the perpetrators? It is because there was never a spiritual intervention on the spiritual bondages that may have been acquired as a result of their childhood experiences, and that problem ultimately manifests with the victim now playing the role of perpetrator.

A child that is sexually molested tends to be a molester when he grows up; likewise a child who is physically abused grows up to be a killer. Modern science claim the perpetrator commits these sins to seek revenge, but these are simple reasons of a drowning man who does not even know that he is drowning. Without the Bible truth, we shall continue singing like the Titanic band that sang until they perished in the merciless sea of social sins.

This analogy is subject to debate and back up with quantifiable data on statistics of murder and the profiles of the perpetrators of such crimes. All I am saying is that a child who is subjected to such physical abuses should be treated as a spiritual patient and administered spiritual prescriptions, rather than address his issues on the surface through psychiatric counseling alone.

All this does not seem fair, and it isn't! Warfare is seldom fair. There is no such thing as a fair fight. Even in carnal warfare, there are a lot of victims who suffer not because they are directly involved in the fighting, but are victims of the battle due to either collateral or incident damage. But our God is a deliverer, who can break such bondages, heal us and restore our sanctity. If the devil is left without a tactical spiritual advantage, he would have to seek elsewhere to carry out his devilish schemes.

"Flee from sexual immorality. All other sins a man commits are outside his body, but he who sins sexually sins against his own body." (1 Corinthians 6:18)

I still maintain that the devil has no authority and power over our lives. He is not omni-potent (all powerful), omniscient (all knowing) and neither is he omni-present (all present). He knows that he cannot stand up and wage a decisive fight with God and his protected children. He therefore identifies or creates gaps or weaknesses in our lives, and concentrates overwhelming spiritual attacks against them. Once he has achieved a penetration, he exploits such opportunities to destroy further the other different spiritual facets of an upright child of God.

Tom's initial weakness was lust. The devil attacked that weakness. That now did not remain the only spiritual problem that Tom suffered. He developed other weaknesses such as drunkenness, nightclub mongering, smoking, and low living. The Bible says that when the devil makes a comeback into a Christian's life, he comes back in full force because he does not want to lose him for the second time again!

"Then it goes and brings along seven other spirits more evil than itself, and they enter and live there; and the last state of that person is worse than the first." (Matthews 12:45)

The devil does not only attack individual Christians, because he also knows that a church is made up of many members. So within the church, he identifies the critical vulnerabilities within the congregation. As I have already alluded to, there are some churches that are not firmly founded on Christ; their hope, their trust, their faith, as well as inspiration are depended upon the church leadership. Attack such figures, and the entire church collapses!

Just as in carnal warfare, the contest is not a contest of an individual against an individual but an organized whole or forces, consisting of manifold echelons and units. The combat of each of these echelons and members form, therefore, a distinct unit. Furthermore, the motive of the fight and its object, form the unit.

Now, to each of these units, which we distinguish in the contest based on their functions and role, we attach the name of the units; infantry, amour, air defense, artillery, air force, engineers, and logistics. All these units fight together as an integrated whole in a combined arms configuration. They individually possess unique sets of capabilities and limitations, and thus by working together they seek to complement each other whilst working towards a common goal.

Anything short of the above truths is a gateway to the demise of whoever engages in combat without this basic operational organization. In spiritual warfare, our ignorance leads to the church or the Christian body operating in such a posture that competes rather than complement with the others.

"I Paul, a prisoner for the Lord, urge you to live in a manner worthy of the call you have received, with all humility and gentleness, with patience, bearing with one another through love, striving to preserve the unity of the spirit through the bond of peace." (Ephesians 4:1)

God's word through Paul outlines the various units that make up this team concept which should complement instead of compete against one another.

"Now there are varieties of gifts, but the same Spirit; and there are varieties of the same services, but the same Lord; and there are varieties of the same activities, but it is the same God who activates all of them in everyone. To each is given the manifestation of the spirit for the common good."

(1 Corinthians 12: 4-11).

The devil knows that by incorporating this wide array of functions, we satisfy the basic integrity of unity in service. He therefore would try his level best to deny us this, and thus it is one of the many reasons of disjointedness among the believers as well as churches throughout the world. Of course some of the perpetrators are doing this fully aware of whom and what they are satisfying, whereas the majorities are acting in utter oblivion.

I have often wondered why some churches would even strive for growth when they are at the same time compromising this basic condition. In the letters of Saint Paul, he talked vehemently about unity to the churches of Corinth, Galatia, Thessalonica, Macedonia, and is still talking to many other churches of the world today.

We teach corporate spirit (or esprit de corps) in every organization. We know very well that this cohesion is a potent formula for the survival of the organization.

The same also holds true even to the church as a body of Christ. No organ is more important than the other; they all directly or indirectly depend on each other in order to effectively and efficiently function. It is the fundamental Christian virtue, and it is more important than anything else.

The primary target and critical vulnerability within the church structure is the church leadership, and that is why it is very critical and crucial that in order for the church to be upright and spiritual, then as the members and the led, we should commit ourselves to pray for the leadership of the church.

Even in the political arena, it is important to pray for our leaders, because a nation without strong and upright leadership is already defeated; it is defeated by hunger and starvation, immorality, racism, incest, greed, corruption, lawlessness, and low productivity.

The information age has created other major challenges that create weaknesses in our spiritual lives, which are easily and expediently exploited by the devil. Have you ever wondered about the potential effects of pornographic or x-rated movies in your spiritual wellbeing? If you are not strong, as I know you are not, then you should stay away from such intellectually deprived, morally decayed, instrument of the devil, designed by some morally decayed, mind-twisted, lost, godless pagans who hate God and moral absolutes.

What do you think influenced the producers of such products to come up with such a perverse psychological weapon that has destroyed many relationships? Believe me, it does not build or improve your character and sexual performance capacity; it tears it apart and so you should stay away from it. It makes us vulnerable to further exploitation of our fidelity by the adversary. This is exactly what the Bible referred to in the book of James 1:14.

*“**But each one is tempted when, by his own evil desire, he is dragged away and enticed.**”*

Movies on their own are one area that the devil asserts his influence, and because we tend to believe that moviemakers and actors are these intelligent and up-right personalities that we worship as our idols in the name of celebrity!

The fact is, if it is rated **SNVL** and is not good for viewing by children, then it probably is not good for our consumption too. The devil meticulously selects each word, each scene, and language with a specific task, purpose, and effect that he wants to impress in peoples’ lives in order to make us vulnerable to his attacks.

Think of the movie **'The Davinci Code'** for example. The content of the movie is simply an electronic propaganda meant to corrupt the gospel of the Virgin Mary and the celibacy of our Lord Jesus Christ. On his web site, the author of the Davinci Code, Mr. Dan Brown makes statements about the historical reliability of his work, and the accuracy of his facts.

In another book that I have read concerning the same issue, titled ‘**The Davinci Deception**,’ the author says that some reviewers of **‘The Davinci Code’** have actually literally praised the literature for its “impeccable” research!

Without other knowledge of the truth, where would anybody in his right senses derive the basis for the 'impeccability' in the book or the movie?

Don't we define *reason* as the process through which the mind forms new statements on the bases of information already known? Again, we define *logic* as the process of attempting to achieve correctness through the process of reasoning! So anybody, without any knowledge of the truth but makes such remarks about such nonsensical literature is not reasoning or making any logical statements. This is my 'nice' way of saying that they are equally dumb as such producers.

This is the ultimate state of affairs that the devil had planned and desired when he guided the producers on every script of the movie. The author of '**The Davinci Deception**' says that one woman, when told that the book was total malarkey, replied by saying "if it were not factual it would not have been published."

One man even said now that he had read the book and watched the movie; he will never set foot in the church again! Right now, there is a real woman in America who is claiming that she is the real descendant of the obtuse Davinci code, what absurdity.

The Bible cautions that a true soldier should not get entangled in civilian affairs. A spiritual warrior should also know his inheritance in Christ. He knows God's promises and does not present himself an easy prey to the lies and deceptions of the enemy, who tries to call these promises and inheritance vanity.

He understands that deception and lies are Satan's language and his most formidable weapon. He also knows that deception and lies constitute the devil's principal defense when he cannot effectively attack the truth about the word of God. Therefore, the spiritual warrior seeks to constantly fortify himself in the understanding of God's truth, which he wears like body armor for protection against the lies of the adversary.

Lastly, as a backdrop, I am still reiterating that as ***the*** church of God, we should never, and can never be shaken by any spiritual forces. It has never happened in Bible history, it is not happening now, and it will never happen anywhere in future. In fact, in the Bible the book of Revelations talks about Jesus as the King of Kings and the Lord of Lords; our triumphant King with a total and eternal victory with his Church, for his Church, in his Church and to his Church; with the total and ***eternal defeat of Satan and his followers.***

The end-times challenges require a church that stands up against Satan and his evil schemes, a church with the quest for conquest guaranteed which is only guaranteed by Jehovah God alone. It requires the congregation which preserves its functional structures even under very severe and adverse spiritual attacks and challenges; a church that maintains its firm stand in Christ Jesus, and never losses its sense of responsibility, duty, and direction.

It requires members that retain their respect for the authority vested upon the church leadership by God, and the members who look at their afflictions and spiritual challenges as the means to the ultimate glory, rather than a curse, which in turn lingers in their lives and stifles spiritual growth and maturity.

Such is the fundamental requirement of the church of Jesus Christ that will stand against the wiles and fiery darts of the adversary, because it is imbued with the spirit of God.

"I consider that the sufferings of this present time are not worth comparing with the glory about to be revealed to us. For the creation waits with eager longing for the revealing of the children of God, for the creation was subjected to futility, not of its own will but by the will of the one who subjected it, in hope that the creation itself will be set free from its bondage to decay and will obtain the freedom of the glory of the children of God."

(Romans 8:18)

CHAPTER 9

CONCLUSION

By concluding, I am not even suggesting that I have covered all that there is to cover, because the examples of how the devil attacks us as the church and children of God are far too numerous to catalogue. Spiritual warfare is not a mathematical exercise; it is a spiritual contest, despite the physical beings that engage in it. It possesses fundamentally intangible nature that simply cannot be fought through physical means.

Unfortunately, in spiritual warfare, the adversary sometimes comes as an angel of life. The devil cannot engage in any direct confrontation with the children of God. The source from where we derive our spiritual strength is Jesus, and so he is aware that any direct confrontation with the armies of God would be absolutely suicidal and could jeopardize his operations.

Make no mistake however, into believing that the devil is a stupid, ugly horned monster that is incapable of victories over Christians. There is no evidence of such in the Bible; in fact, as I have earlier indicated, the devil was the most brilliant angel; most intelligent, most witty; just anything that would describe the highest mental faculty of man. He was also the most gorgeous, most handsome, hunk of a man!

I believe that by understanding, above most, how our adversary fights can serve as spiritual caution and help us maintain situational awareness of his scams. Lastly, the devil is not skillful by the definition; he is simply an ***opportunist***.

"But they that wait for Jehovah shall renew their strength; they shall mount up with wings as eagles; they shall run, and not be weary; they shall walk, and not faint." (Isaiah 40:31)

As Christians, we should triumph against every situation with the hope assured through the gospel of Jesus Christ through Saint Paul, in that ***'For us, to live is Christ and to die is gain'*** (Philippians 1:21). We should smile at the spiritual storms in our lives just as the eagle smiles at the imminent adverse weather and soars without any obvious hindrance. It is said that an eagle has a natural ability to know when a storm is approaching even long before the storm breaks.

The eagle will fly to some high spot and wait for the winds to come. When the storm hits, it sets out its wings so that the wind will pick it up and lift it above the storm. While the storm rages below, the eagle is soaring above it. The eagle does not avoid confronting the storm; it simply uses the storm to lift it higher. It rises on the winds that bring the storm.

This is the reason why God allows us to go through such challenges in our spiritual lives, so that we develop the sure-footedness as we await our glory unspeakable. With Jesus in our life boat, we too should smile at the storm because we know that it shall bring us no harm but good.

"Fear not, for I have redeemed you; I have summoned you by name; you are Mine. When you pass through the waters, I will be with you; and when you pass through the rivers, they will not sweep over you. When you walk through the fire, you will not be burned; the flames will not set you ablaze. For I am the Lord your God, the Holy One of Israel, your Savior..." (Isaiah 43:1-3)

The battle is raging on, and there shall not be any cease-fire, until the day our Lord comes to cast Satan and all his hosts to the bottom of the bottomless pit.

As for me, my military service in the Army of my country shall in the very near future come to an end. However, throughout my entire life on this earth, I intend to remain a soldier in the Army of My God until the day I am relieved of my duties. Faith, Prayer and the Word of God shall remain my weapons of Warfare.

I am being trained and taught by the Holy Spirit, developed in proficiency by experience, tried and tested by adversity, and am undergoing spiritual proficiency tests by fire. One day, soon and very soon, I shall be honored with a crown of glory with Jesus in person as the great chancellor. I am a happy and rewarded volunteer in this Army, and I am enlisted for eternity. I will either retire in this Army at the rapture of the church, or die in this Army; otherwise I will not resign or retire, go Absent Without Official Leave (A.W.O.L), or shirk my duties.

I will not be subverted by world affairs. With God as my Commander-in-Chief, Jesus as my Army Commander, the Holy Spirit as my Executive Officer, and the Bible as my survival kit, I am pressing on as I do the double time. My service in His Army is not in vain (1 Corinthians. 15:58), because one day when my Commander calls me from this warfare, He will promote me to the highest rank and then bring me back to rule this world with Him.

May God richly bless everyone who reads this book, and may we stay encouraged because we are more than conquerors through Christ our Lord. May His name forever be praised and glorified.

(Romans 8:37)

BIBLIOGRAPHY

- **Benny Hinn**-Good Morning Holy Spirit
- **R. Leonhard** -The Art of Maneuver
- **Carl von Clausewitz** -On War
- **Sun Tzu** -The Art of War
- **Holy Bible** -New Revised Version
- **Encyclopedia of Warfare**

www.ingramcontent.com/pod-product-compliance
Ingram Content Group UK Ltd.
Pitfield, Milton Keynes, MK11 3LW, UK
UKHW041846190726
13854UKWH00002B/752

9 781425 106485